Successful School Change and Transition for the Child with Asperger Syndrome

by the same author

How to Make School Make Sense
A Parents' Guide to Helping the Child with Asperger Syndrome
Foreword by Tony Atwood
ISBN 978 1 84310 664 7

of related interest

Making the Move
A Guide for Schools and Parents on the Transfer of Pupils with Autism Spectrum Disorders (ASDs) from Primary to Secondary School
K.I. Al-Ghani and Lynda Kenward
Illustrated by Haitham Al-Ghani
ISBN 978 1 84310 934 1

Choosing a School for a Child with Special Needs
Ruth Birnbaum
ISBN 978 1 84310 987 7

Hints and Tips for Helping Children with Autism Spectrum Disorders
Useful Strategies for Home, School, and the Community
Dion E. Betts and Nancy J. Patrick
ISBN 978 1 84310 896 2

Successful School Change and Transition for the Child with Asperger Syndrome

A Guide for Parents

Clare Lawrence

Jessica Kingsley Publishers
London and Philadelphia

First published in 2010
by Jessica Kingsley Publishers
116 Pentonville Road
London N1 9JB, UK
and
400 Market Street, Suite 400
Philadelphia, PA 19106, USA

www.jkp.com

Copyright © Clare Lawrence 2010

Library of Congress Cataloging in Publication Data
A CIP catalogue record for this book is available from the Library of Congress

British Library Cataloguing in Publication Data
A CIP catalogue record for this book is available from the British Library

ISBN 978 1 84905 052 4

Printed and bound in Great Britain by
Page Bros (Norwich) Ltd

This book is dedicated to the memory of
Douglas Gott,
my father,
with all love and gratitude.

Acknowledgements

I would like to offer my thanks to everyone who has helped me gather the material for this book, in particular to the staff at the various schools I have visited. I am aware of how busy all teachers are, always, and I am very grateful for your time.

Away from schools, I have received generous help and advice from many other professionals. My particular thanks to Seonaid Anderson, King's College, London; Marianna Murin, Great Ormond Street Hospital and Dr Luke Beardon, Sheffield Hallam University.

Finally, my gratitude goes – as ever – to Claire Thorley and to everyone at St Gilbert's.

Contents

Foreword

Transitions often cause great anxiety for both children and adults on the autism spectrum, and parents and others have to work hard to reduce this. The move to a new secondary school is one of the greatest challenges that pupils have to face, and for children with Asperger syndrome (AS) the worry caused to parents and children alike can be considerable. In recognition of this, there is a growing body of literature and transition toolkits specifically for children on the autism spectrum. This book by Clare Lawrence, herself the mother of a boy with AS, is a very welcome addition to this literature.

As Clare points out, parents are not present in school to 'look out' for their child and they often worry during the day about what might be happening and whether problems are being noticed and addressed. Clare has written very much from a parent's perspective, sharing her own experiences and knowledge on what can make a positive difference. She also draws on her work as an advisory teacher, describing incidents and strategies observed in schools.

Although the book is written for parents, Clare stresses the importance of working effectively with school staff and other professionals. She makes the important point that children with AS differ from one another and that good knowledge about the individual child and his needs and strengths are paramount. As parents know their child best, they are well placed to share information and strategies with the school and should be encouraged by schools to do so.

Clare has her own particular experience of her son's transition, but has generalized beyond this to show that issues which affect one child might not affect another and that a bank of strategies needs to be drawn upon. On the whole, the book is written in a way which encourages creativity and offers a range of ideas, not being overly prescriptive on what a parent or school should do.

There is a whole section in the book on analyzing what has worked to date in the child's current school in terms of strategies and successes, and ways in which to enhance and maintain self-esteem. Some areas of school life to be considered are the rules and regulations and the potential sensory challenges to the child in terms of smells, sounds or lighting, for example. Skills needed to function within the school are identified (e.g. telling the time, queuing, using the canteen, travelling to school). Some strategies suggested include having a safe haven, a named person, the use of a lap-top computer, and having an Exit Card. Advances in technology with e-mails, mobile phones and texting means that communication can be more immediate and effective for parents, staff and the child.

There is a very useful chapter which gives suggestions on what parents might do during the holidays prior to transition. This suggests rehearsing particular routines and journeys. The book ends with a check-list which effectively serves as a summary to the book – giving 20 areas which need to be considered to ensure a successful transition to a new school.

To conclude, AS is often called a hidden condition as the difficulties and anxieties experienced may not be obvious to others. Some children have said they 'pretend to be normal' and do not know to tell staff that they are feeling upset or distressed. In addition, their facial expression and body language may not reflect their emotions and distress. Clare makes the point that there is a danger in staff thinking that no sign of difficulty means that all is well and that the placement is successful. We need to check this out by asking the child directly. Many biographies of adults with AS describe the loneliness, rejection, fear and anxiety they experienced at school – none of which was noticed by staff around them. This very readable book should help the needs of children with AS to be made visible so that their anxieties are recognized and addressed.

Dr Glenys Jones
Autism Centre for Education and Research
University of Birmingham
September 2009

Introduction

Changing school can be difficult for anyone. Children worry about making new friends, about getting lost, about doing the wrong thing and not 'fitting in'. They worry that they won't be able to do the work, that they'll fall behind with homework or that they'll get into trouble for doing the wrong thing. Parents worry that they will fall in with the 'wrong crowd', that they'll fail to achieve academically or that they'll fail to take the opportunities available to them. School is a challenge that children face away from their parents, and that can add to the stress for both parties.

For the child with Asperger syndrome (AS), and for his parents, the challenge of changing schools is even greater. The child with AS entering a mainstream school enters what is likely to be, to all intents and purposes, an alien environment. It is an environment peopled by those who may not understand the child, and not be able to see things in the same way as him. (I say 'him'; autism and AS affect both boys and girls, but for ease of understanding I will use 'him' for the child unless referring to issues specifically affecting girls, and 'her' for teachers and support staff.) It is an environment that is governed by rules that may be unintelligible, is filled with sensory stimuli that may be hard to manage and that uses a language that has little meaning. It may be a very frightening place indeed.

For the parents of the child with AS, sending their child into this environment can be traumatic. We may be desperate to help our child, but feel powerless to know how to do so. Schools may feel like closed, almost mysterious institutions. We remember them, with a certain childish slant, from when we attended them ourselves, but we are aware of how much they have changed since then. They are busy places, moving along to their own timetables and having their own hierarchies and structures. They are mini-societies in their own right, and ones of which we, as parents, may feel we have no part. Schools are where children go to get away from their parents. Given that, how can we help our vulnerable children better to survive?

This book is about ways that we can help. We as parents of children with AS, of children with conditions on the autistic spectrum, are hugely important in the education of those children. We can provide the factor of consistency. We who are the child's parents, or who have assumed that parental responsibility, need to provide continuity and cohesion in the child's journey to adulthood. We know him best. When he is in transition between one school and the next, we need to provide the security to help him to manage that transition.

That is not to say that the schools don't have a role too. Many schools have strong school transition programmes in place for all their students, and most will provide extra support for a child with special educational needs. The purpose of this book is not to undermine these programmes, but to help parents to support them and to participate in them more fully. A child with AS is going to make the transition from one school to the next most smoothly if all the parties involved – the old school, the new school, the parents and the child himself – are all involved fully. It is also the case that change of school can happen for many reasons, not just routinely as the child becomes older. Clearly if the move is because of relocation, and the new school is at the opposite side of the country, this will limit the practical transition support that the schools can offer. In a case like this, it is even more important that parents feel confident that they can support their child in this move themselves.

In general terms, this book deals with transitions that occur in the middle of a child's education, for example from primary to secondary school, from elementary to middle or high. The reason these sorts of levels are being focused upon is because, as the child gets older, greater independence is expected, and parental influence may be less encouraged. If your child is moving from nursery school to first school, much of what is in this book will still be relevant, but it is also the case that you will be far more fully involved in the day-to-day management of your child. It is as the child with AS grows older, and as his peers begin to function independently and without support, that many of the problems around AS and school intensify. This book aims to help parents to support their child with AS, even at the age where parental support is not so usual. Your child with AS is going to continue to need support long after his peers appear self-sufficient. Above all, he is going to need to be supported to manage his AS for himself. It is important to understand that your continued involvement is as much to help him to manage his AS as it is to help him to manage school.

Schools are places of learning. If your child has special educational needs it may be that he has been participating in all manner of support programmes. Perhaps he has been having support with reading or writing skills, with numeracy, or indeed with social and communication skills. If so, the feedback on these programmes, together with all the assessments and details of his progress, will be forwarded to his new school. Unfortunately, this information may make you feel even more helpless. It may be presented in a way that makes no sense to you, filled with incomprehensible numbers and acronyms. If so, although it is of course perfectly reasonable to ask that this information is made clearer to you, you should not be made to feel that you 'know less' about your child's needs. You may not be up to date with current education intervention strategy, but you know your child. You know that if he is forced to sit near the bin containing apple-cores from break time, he will feel so sick he will be unable to take in any information whatsoever. You know that he will be able to hear, and is likely to be distressed by, the whine of the interactive whiteboard. You know that he needs to be given clear, specific instructions to get changed for sports. You know how tired and distraught he can be after managing a stressful day at school, and you know just how much work and support it is going to take to make his move to a new school successful. Your child's teachers and specialist support staff have a wealth of knowledge, professional expertise and experience that they can bring to bear to help that transition, but you know your child. You are going to have to find a way to all work together as effectively as possible if the move is going to work smoothly.

This book looks at ways to facilitate that working together, and particularly looks at ways that you, as parents, can support your child. It is divided into sections covering the period from before you make the move, through the break between schools and on until after the move is safely behind you. It aims to provide a 'road map' for you to use to guide your child through this potentially challenging time and, it is hoped, out to the other side. I hope it helps.

It is worth saying though, that just as at the end of the book (Appendix: Transition Check-list) I say that no school can be expected to have all the supports suggested here in place, so the same should be said of parents. Parents (all parents) have tremendous pressures and responsibilities, and for the parents of a child with AS, these are multiplied many times. Many of us feel bewildered and exhausted by the many battles we have had to fight on behalf of our child, and we may still be reeling from receiving the diagnosis. We may feel that we have the double pressure of 'jumping through the hoops' to get the support available for our child's education, and yet at the same time be fighting that same system to try to make that support better. Although we look for ways to help our child, we may feel overwhelmed when various well-meaning advisers or pressure groups (or books such as this one) seem to suggest that we should do so much more than we feel able to achieve.

What we must bear in mind is that not only are all children with AS different, but so are all parents, all families and, of course, all schools. No school, pupil or family could or should provide all the support suggested in this book. Such support is unlikely to be needed, and is likely to result in burn-out by all parties. What can be a help, though, is to understand the various options and to pick and choose those few that are going to help your child in your situation. One or two solid strategies, consistently and successfully applied, can make all the difference during this transition process, and may be all that is needed to tip the balance over into success.

Your child, and you, are not alone. Many, many pupils with AS make the transition between schools every year. Some will manage without a hitch. Others will experience some degree of difficulty, and the resources and suggestions given here should help through the bumpier times. Nor will your child make the transition alone. You as parents are just part of the network of support, including the staff at his old school and various education and autistic spectrum disorder (ASD) experts as well as the staff at his new school, who will help during this period. For you as well as for your child, it may feel that you are losing the friends and helpers who have 'looked after' your child during his education so far. You are not really losing them; they are just becoming different people.

This book looks at ways to tackle the problems, and problems there may be (or you wouldn't be reading this). However, one way to use this book is to go through it saying to yourself, 'Our child doesn't need that; he managed fine with that situation; we never felt worried about that...' While it is really important that we, and those around our child, appreciate just how difficult this move may be for a child with AS, it is essential that we stay focused on that child as an individual. What we must all not forget to notice and celebrate, is just how well he is managing it.

1

Planning the Move

1.1 Identifying the problem

Before we can begin to address the question of how best to support our child with Asperger syndrome (AS) in moving school, we need to be clear why there is a problem. Surely all children are a little anxious about moving schools, but they usually cope pretty well once the move takes place. Why is the child with AS so different?

First of all, acceptance that he *is* different is key. Because AS is a hidden condition, it can be difficult for the neuro-typical (i.e. non-autistic) mind to get itself round just how differently the person with AS perceives the world. It is helpful if we try to keep in mind that this difference is much greater than we may understand. The person with AS may hear the world differently, see it differently, be overwhelmed by tastes, smells and sensation that we may barely perceive. Perhaps more confusing, he may not understand the actions of the people around him. Many of the verbal and non-verbal clues given off by people may not be interpretable by him. He may find it incredibly difficult to process the information that is likely to bombard him. Much of it may simply not 'add up' in his mind, and he may not be able to make the mental leaps and connections needed to process this information into a cohesive whole. He may lack the communication skills to be able to articulate his confusion or to find the answer to his questions, and may be unable to rely on the kind of 'collective understanding' that his peers are using. They will learn as much from watching each other, copying what others do, interpreting, perhaps, a teacher's reaction to another pupil and using that interpretation to predict what they should do. The pupil with AS may not be able to tap into this source of understanding, and without this understanding may find a his new environment a very confusing place indeed.

Because change is confusing, many people with AS rely on routine. A way of doing things that has been built up and found to work may be very precious, and the person may be reluctant, or even unable, to let that familiarity go. This fear of change and reliance on routine mean that the approaching transfer to another school, which is change on just about every level, is likely to provoke considerable anxiety.

In addition, a transfer to another school is not just going to be about learning a new version of his current environment. Changing schools is usually about growing up, and growing up involves a whole new set of rules, particularly social ones. It also demands greater independence, and provides less and less opportunity for support from the traditional sources of parents and family. There is likely to be less support available, also, in school. Instead of one teacher, your child is likely to be faced with ten or twelve different teachers a week, each teaching a different subject and having different styles, expectations and rules. Instead of one classroom, he may be faced with the challenge of repeated movement from place to place, from room to room. Each room will have different lighting, different smells, different background noise. In each, he has to work out where to sit and to try to predict what will happen next…and that's after he's actually found the room! First he will have to negotiate a confusing labyrinth of stairs and corridors, each perhaps populated to overflowing by a heaving mass of pushing, jostling humanity. He has to learn a whole new set of rules, and to accept that some of these rules at least may not be obeyed by other pupils around him.

Growing up, of course, involves much more than just increased challenges at school. Puberty brings changes in a young person's body, and may be a source of anxiety in itself. It is a time of uncertainty and volatile changes in mood, a time where self-image becomes tremendously important and when one's relationships with others, with those of the same and those of the opposite sex, become very important.

These relationship issues may be particularly difficult and confusing for the young person with AS, who may lack the social dexterity to navigate through the minefield that is puberty. He will experience the physical changes and desires of puberty just as his neuro-typical peers will do, but is unlikely to have the skills necessary to handle the shifting relationships and interactions of this time. Adolescents can be very self-absorbed, and few may have the self-confidence themselves to make allowances for 'differentness' in another person at this time. The young person with AS who finds someone attractive may not understand the complex interchange of signals that govern the next move in the relationships 'ballet', and in getting it wrong may risk ridicule and rejection. He may even find himself facing accusations of stalking or sexual harassment if he fails to interpret signals correctly. It can be a very difficult time.

Schools vary enormously in their levels of understanding of the condition of AS, and indeed in to what extent they take their pastoral responsibilities for their young people seriously. Even if a school has a strong disability or special educational needs policy, this may not be carried forward to every teacher and every lesson. Training for teachers in autistic spectrum disorders (ASDs) remains patchy, and it is unfortunately a fact that teachers have many other concerns on their minds than that of managing the needs of one child with AS. If the teacher is struggling to keep order, to meet the learning needs of her whole range of students, to get her message across and to get her students through exams with sufficiently high grades, she may have little time or energy left to really work to understand the needs of your child with AS.

That is why this book is aimed at parents. You know your child, and you are motivated to focus on your child. There is a great deal that you can do to help your child through this transition, and in doing so to empower your child to manage his AS for himself. Your child will grow into an adolescent with AS, and then into an adult with AS. The AS remains a constant, and as well as dealing with the changing demands of being a child, an adolescent, a young adult, you will need to help him to deal with the demands of his AS.

There is much that can help you. For a start, you can use the check-list in the Appendix to identify what your child's new school is providing and how. Where you find that provision is not available, you can use the same resource as a shopping list. Which of the provisions outlined do you believe would help your child through this transition? Who should you ask to get them put in place? How can you help to ensure that they are provided? Which of them can you provide for your child yourself?

You may find that much of what is suggested is in place, and your awareness of it merely strengthens your child's chances of being helped by these provisions. Your child is most unlikely to be the first with AS through the doors of the school. With luck the school will have already built up a good bank of knowledge and expertise. It may be able to provide you with a thriving AS community already present in the school, and a network of parents to help and support you.

Be aware, though, that provision for children with ASDs in schools is only improving slowly. It may be that previous failures to meet the needs of students with this diagnosis have disheartened the school staff. If a previous student with AS has been perceived as disruptive or aggressive, you may have some work to do to educate the school that their lack of meeting that student's needs were likely to be as much or more at fault than the student himself. Getting the school to understand that they should put accommodations in place *before* the need for them becomes obvious may be a time-consuming task.

Your preparation for this turbulent time ahead, and your readiness to be fully engaged in the process, will both help enormously in smoothing the path for your child with AS. You cannot, of course, put all things right. You can, though, be prepared, have strategies in place, be knowledgeable and confident about what you can ask for and provide your child with the reassurance that someone, at least, is in command of the situation and can make this move make sense.

1.2 Planning ahead – the '2-year plan'

It can be hard to decide just how far ahead to plan for our children with AS. Sometimes, in our more anxious moments, we may find ourselves planning years ahead, worrying about provision into adulthood and setting up schemes in our heads for employment, for independent living, even for care into old age. Clearly, although our concerns for our children on into their future lives is genuine, there is a limit to the amount of influence we have on such things now. On the other hand, sometimes a kind of paralysis sets in. Perhaps we have fought long and hard to get a proper diagnosis. Perhaps we then again fought long and hard to set up his current schooling. It can be hard to pick ourselves up yet again and face more battles for schooling at the next stage. As parents of a child with AS we can become, frankly, tired out.

The balance between looking too far ahead, and not looking far enough, seems to be to plan about two years ahead for your child's change of school, if your circumstances allow. Clearly if your move is because of a change of location due to job promotion, redundancy, etc., then this may not happen, but if it is a routine move to the next stage of schooling, it is possible and manageable in this time-scale. This ideal will give one 'quiet' year in which to do the background work, research schools, check out provision, etc. and then one 'active' year when you put all the necessary transition support into place.

If you can draw yourself out a 2-year plan, marking on the various dates and deadlines (both external, for example deadlines to apply for school places and also internal as with your own dates by which you want to complete various stages of research), this should enable you to pace yourself and to keep the business of helping your child move schools clear in your mind in a calm, orderly way. You are going to have to set the confident tone of this move very much for your child. It is essential that you stay on top of any concerns – not to say panics – so that you don't transmit your uncertainties to your child.

Another advantage of the 2-year plan is that you can follow the school year through with the 'safety net' of another year at the current school beyond. Therefore it is possible to begin looking at strategies for smooth transition, and see what works best for your child, while the transition is only the relatively small one of moving up to the final year of the current school. This is the time to look out for things that might go wrong. Does your child get particularly concerned about finding his way to a new room? Is he particularly upset by, for example, having to use different bathrooms or different lockers? Is he relying very heavily on a familiar and trusted support assistant, who will not be able to move with him to the new school in the following year? The transition one year ahead of the big school move is a great opportunity for a 'dry run', and to anticipate future problems and concerns.

It is also an opportunity for you as parent to begin to request that supports be put in place for your child. If you can have transition support written into your child's transition plan now, then that gives plenty of opportunity to develop and fine-tune it ready for the bigger move. By raising the issue of transition support now you are indicating to your child's school that this is a matter that you are approaching actively, and one with which you are requesting active support.

Finally, you can take advantage of this year of relative calm when your child is not facing imminent transition to find out all you can about the environment to which he is ultimately moving. Find out amongst your friends and associates someone whose child is moving up this year. Find out from that child what it is really like. What are the problems, the difficulties, the rewards? What is challenging and different about the new school? What advice can the student give? At the end of the day, it is only a student at a school who *really* knows what it is like to go there. This is your opportunity to put in your research so that you are well placed next year as you prepare your child for the experience.

1.3 Choosing the new school

Depending on where you live, on your country and even on your district, it may be that there is little decision to be made as to which school your child goes to (in that all children in your area attend the same local school) or that it is a huge decision, with a wide and confusing range of choices. As the parent of a child with AS you may be faced with a wider choice than that facing parents of neuro-typical children. Can you request a specific mainstream school? Is there, perhaps, a special school or unit near you? If so, is it Asperger specific, or a more generic 'special education' facility? Is your child eligible to attend? Even if he is, is it where you would most like him to go? What are your criteria for deciding what is going to be 'best' for your child?

These are big questions, and daunting ones. Sometimes the sheer pressure on us as parents, the magnitude of the damage if we 'get it wrong' can be more than we can cope with. We need advice, but sadly that advice is not always as readily available as it should be.

On the other hand, we may find ourselves bombarded by too much advice, and this may not be helpful either. Your child's current school, for example, may have had a child with AS in a previous year who has gone on to thrive at a certain school, and may strongly advise this for your child. Similarly, local autism professionals may have a 'chosen route' that they advise you along. While, clearly, listening to all advice is a good idea, it is good also to remember that you don't have to act on it. Your child is different. All children are different, and a child with AS may be more different than similar to another child, even one who shares his diagnosis. As parents we can be made to feel 'less expert' than the professionals, but we are not. We know our child, and we know our family. Your concerns may be nothing that would even have occurred to professionals advising you about your child with AS. If a school is difficult to get to, for example, that is a valid concern for your family. It is important to be practical, to look at the long-term consequences of the various options and to consider all members of the family. Perhaps the long daily journey to 'School A' would mean that your other children would be spending long periods in the car daily, or long periods in before or after school care. This concern need not rule out 'School A' if you really feel it to be the best option for your child with AS, but nevertheless the concern is worth considering. You need to look after all the members of your family...including yourself.

While it is important, therefore, to seek out all the advice you can get, it is important also to keep an open mind. For advice try the school and the health professionals certainly, but don't forget other parents, both of children with AS and of those without, and those who have tried the school from the inside. Talking to students who go there, or have done so until recently, can be invaluable. Were they happy? Were they aware of bullying? What is their attitude towards people with differences? If you have a chance to meet teachers at the school socially, this can be another way to find out the 'true story'. Statistically, it is likely that mainstream teachers will have had previous experience with children with AS in their classes. How have those experiences been? Are they positive and excited by the experience, or do they talk only in terms of needing more support. Do you feel your 'different' child is going to be truly welcome at the school, whatever the official line may be?

All schools will have an inclusion and/or disability policy, and this is well worth scrutinizing. It is best to keep in mind, though, that there may be a gap between the ideal best policy, as laid down in the prospectus, and what is actually happening on a day-to-day level. Official documents can be all very interesting, but nothing is going to replace going into a school, several times if you wish, and getting a feel for it. Are you made welcome? Do the children seem happy? Do you enjoy your visits? If you don't, do you really want to tie yourself to this establishment, and submit your vulnerable child to it for years to come?

Walking past the school at the beginning or end of a school day can tell you a lot about it too, as can catching buses or trains used by the students. Headteachers are forever emphasizing to students that they are 'ambassadors for their school' as they travel around their local community. They go on about it because it's true! If the students spill out of the school gates at the end of the day pushing and swearing, this may tell you something, particularly through their use of language. If the students are name-calling, and particularly if they are using discriminatory language, whether that be racial, sexual or disability orientated, that can be an indication of the underlying social ethos of what is acceptable to them (the school may have an official policy that outlaws discrimination, but that may nevertheless not translate itself to how the students really feel and act). How is your child with AS going to fare in this environment?

Your first duty to your child is, arguably, to keep him safe. Children do not have fewer rights than adults, nor people with AS fewer than those without. All people as a basic right should be able to go about their day free from threat or intimidation, from violence and from verbal assault. Because of his AS, your child may be more vulnerable to these dangers than other people, and because of his age may be less able to avoid them (because you compel him to go to school) than an adult would. It is for you to ensure that the school environment you choose for him is a safe one. Of course, what you are looking for is something that will be a great deal more than this minimum, but will be somewhere that will help your child to grow, to learn, to develop and to mature. The experience of school can have a huge effect on all people, those with AS included. You want the experience to be more than merely 'safe'. This is the community environment that you are going to trust to help your child grow up. You will want it to help him fulfil his potential, to learn positive values and to help him on his road to knowing 'who he is'. You are looking for something pretty special.

I believe that such schools do exist, and that the school experience for the student with AS can be enriching and worthwhile. I do think also that finding that environment, and indeed helping to create it where it is lacking, is hard work. As the parent of a child with AS you may have your work cut out!

1.4 Involving wider autism professionals

Having said that autism professionals must not be allowed to make you feel 'less expert' about your child's and your family's needs, there is still, of course, much that they can offer. For one thing, they will know the wider autism environment in which they work, so they will know which schools are 'AS friendly' and which are not. Although I would be cautious about accepting health professionals' assertion that a school is 'right' for your child with AS, without checking it out for yourself, I would be equally cautious about dismissing health professionals' advice that a school is 'wrong'. Such professionals may not be free to tell you the whole truth, and it may be that they know that the headteacher is autism-hostile (it has been known) and that you will be facing an up-hill struggle if you send your child there. That doesn't make it right, and it doesn't mean you shouldn't fight prejudice when you meet it – but you should at least be forewarned.

Health professionals are also in a strong position to offer training to schools and to improve lack of AS understanding. They may be able to support your child into the school and to provide AS-appropriate education. They will also be more strongly placed than you may be to offer suggestions, for example the requirement for a low-stimulus safe haven, and to have their explanations for the reasons for this accepted. One of the biggest challenges you face is getting your child's behaviour to be understood. Autism professionals may be able to help spread the understanding that your child's behaviour is not 'challenging' for no reason, is not 'naughty' nor 'attention seeking' but that it is meaningful. Understanding the reasons behind autistic behaviours, and finding ways to support or remedy those reasons, is vitally important for your child to thrive in his new school environment. Anyone who can support and develop that understanding has got to be helpful.

1.5 Preparing your child

When you are pretty much secure in your own mind about which school your child will be moving to, you are in a position to begin involving him in preparations for that move. You may feel that it has been unfair to exclude him from these discussions up until now. However, given the uncertainty and anxiety which making decisions can produce in people with AS, it may actually have been unfair to involve him too early. Unless you really are going to let his opinions influence your decision right from the beginning (even if his opinions seem to you to be based on irrelevant considerations), it may be better to shelter him until you are more sure yourself of the likely direction you will be taking.

When you have a 'shortlist' of schools that each has merit, this is an ideal time for your child to become involved. He may well respond better to the whole process if he feels that his opinion has been properly considered – after all, he will ultimately be the one most affected by the decision. However, you may need to be cautious about ways you involve him. It is important to be specific about what you are looking for when you read prospectuses, look at websites and indeed visit the school itself. Your child may be 'put off' an otherwise excellent school by things you would not consider. Perhaps he will refuse to consider a school because of a smell in the corridor, perhaps because there was dog mess on the driveway, perhaps because a piece of work displayed on one of the walls contained an uncorrected error. These are valid considerations for your child, but they are not necessarily considerations you would use in making your decision. By being very specific about what you are looking at with your child (perhaps with a check-list of questions which reflect what is important to him: are there sufficient computers? Are there lunch time clubs? Is there a Quiet Room?) you should be able to stay focused on finding the best school for him.

The other danger with involving your child with AS too soon in this process is that things change. Perhaps the school you favour is one that is particularly difficult to get into. Perhaps you will need to wait to hear if he has secured a place. Perhaps your own family circumstances may change, for example with a change of job or because of family illness. Generally it is best to wait and involve your child in the transition to the next school when you are able to limit the variables. Nothing is more likely to get the transition process off to a poor start with a child with AS than to have to change your mind when you, and he, have made your choice.

Once you have finalized where he is going, and absorbed many of the stresses and worries about where that will be yourself (and protected him from them), it is time to fully involve him in the transition process. Given the limitations already discussed, this should be done in plenty of time to ensure that he has the time to deal with the transition. How long ahead of the move will depend on individual circumstances (some schools or education authorities do not confirm a place until very late in the academic year), but it should be within the final year and, if at all possible, with a good few months still to go.

A good way of approaching this business is to create a transition plan to share with your child. As discussed earlier (see section 1.2), you may have started this when you began the process of choosing a school place, and it is helpful if you can extend this now to include your son or daughter. Such transition plans are more usually associated with the move for people with AS from children's to adult services. In this context they are detailed plans that look at what the individual will need into the future and which involve him in the decisions regarding that future, together with the various other agencies involved. Critically, they concern not only *what* needs to be done, but also *who* will be responsible for doing it. As such, they are equally relevant for the transition between schools.

Your transition plan is going to evolve over the next few months and its focus is going to change. It is most useful if it can be a document that reassures your child, and is a visual reminder that there is a plan, that everything is in order and that the school change is not going to leave him in some sort of limbo. It should provide the structure for him to articulate his worries and concerns, and be somewhere where you can record what is being done to address those concerns. It will show what is happening, and what is going to happen next. Managed successfully, this transition plan is going to be the 'visual lifebelt' which keeps your child afloat throughout this potentially difficult period.

How you present the plan will depend on you, and on your child's age and style. He may prefer anything from a computer document to a flip chart, from a neatly managed calendar to a marker-pen-emboldened length of wallpaper. Whatever you use, it needs to be in a form which is flexible. It is never likely to be just one document, but rather something which evolves and changes as time moves on.

Rather like zooming in from a satellite picture, the plan needs to move from the broad view down to the specific. To begin with it may be something as simple as a document which reads 'Leaves "X" school (month and year) : Holidays : Begin "Y" school (month and year)'. Gradually, as you continue through this book, that skeleton will begin to be fleshed out and (it is hoped) become more and more useful as the process evolves.

2

Before Moving On

2.1 Collecting your data. What has worked up to now?

Perhaps most important, before your child moves away from his current environment, is to collect as much of the information, expertise and downright success that has occurred so far. If your child has been in his current school for some time there should, it would be hoped, be a wealth of strategies and techniques to help him that have been built up. What's more, these will have been built up by a whole array of people – by his teachers, of course, and by his learning aides or support assistants if he has had them, but also by his fellow pupils and perhaps most importantly of all by himself. Your child has worked out strategies to cope with his current environment, and these strategies must not be lost.

A good way to start is to make a list with your child of potential problems and stumbling blocks associated with a typical day at school (i.e. his current school), that occur because of your child's Asperger syndrome (AS). For example:

Sometimes I have problems because I:

1. worry

2. find it difficult to recognize people

3. miss/don't understand verbal instructions

4. feel 'overloaded' (sensory)

5. shout/hit out/'lose it'

6. don't know what to do at break time

7. don't like eating with/in front of other people

8. need 'time out' to think my own thoughts

9. find it hard to stay organized

10. find it difficult to get heard/communicate.

Make your list as personal as possible for your child, and make sure that you get an opportunity to allow as many people as possible to add into it. Your child's teachers may well have things to add that you were not even aware of, and your child himself may have issues that neither you nor his teachers had considered (number 10 on this list came from our Sam. We and his teachers all thought we were giving him opportunities to be heard, but that's not how he sees it!). Having made your list, go back and write beside it how that issue is being resolved. Some issues the teachers will have specific strategies for (behavioural problems, for example, may cover a whole range of things but should, most usefully, indicate what more appropriate ways of expressing frustration or distress have been found to work). Other issues may have been resolved by your child himself, for example recognizing teachers by voice rather than by facial feature. It is important to keep firmly in mind that this list is about *solutions*, not about *problems*. These are issues that have been resolved, at least in part, and it is these ways of resolving them that you are keen to record. After all, the problems may not reoccur at the new school (for example, the new school may not have trumpet lessons going on in the room next door to the one in which your child does Art), but the resolutions are still important. If your child was allowed to wear headphones and listen to white noise in the example above, this solution may well be a useful one to bear in mind. So, for example:

Sometimes I have problems because I:

1. worry…so I try to remember to record my worries in my book and go through them (and find solutions) with my parents or my counsellor

2. find it difficult to recognize people…so I wait until they speak and then I can recognize their voice

3. miss/don't understand verbal instructions…so Mrs M often gives me a separate written worksheet or lesson plan.

You are collecting expertise on your child, and as such it should be a positive exercise for all concerned. It is also helping you to begin to formulate some positive strategies to share with his new school. It has got to be better to arrive with solutions rather than problems whenever you approach a new venture. Finally, this list is a great place to add in your child's skills and strengths, and to record how his current school have nurtured and encouraged them. One of the dangers for a child with 'special needs' is that everyone will concentrate on the challenges, and will miss all the positives that he has to offer. Whether your child is very bright, has a particularly good memory, is a voracious reader, or has an encyclopaedic knowledge of bug species, this is a chance to record it and how his school have made it work to his advantage. If your child hates waste, now is an opportunity to record his contribution to the recycling record of the school. If he has been spending break times indoors rather than managing the chaos of the school yard, perhaps he has used that time to help reorganize the library or the stock cupboards. If you are to share information about your child, you need to balance his needs with his achievements. After all, if you can actively celebrate all the good things he has achieved at his current school, that is passing the message to the new school both that you have high expectations and also that you are appreciative. Your new relationship with the school is, arguably, going to be almost as influential on whether he succeeds or not as your child's own relationship. It does no harm to show right from the start that you understand and value good work when it occurs.

It may well be useful to record this positive information, also, in a list. The two lists together will form a fair indication of both his strengths and his needs. The list of positives helps focus your child's mind on all the many things that he does well and that he has achieved. The list will, of course, be highly individual, but might look something like this:

I am good at:

1. Science (or Technology or Music or whatever)

2. being 'reliable'

3. doing visual presentations about subjects that interest me

4. using ICT

5. working from a book/worksheet

6. remembering to switch lights and appliances off and to save electricity

7. following the rules

8. helping in the library

9. using my 'Angry Card' rather than hitting out

10. remembering details.

This second list not only gives you a useful tool for maintaining your child's self-esteem by reminding him of the things that he *can* do, it also – taken side-by-side with his list of problems – begins to provide a blue-print for him and for his future school on strategies that work for him. So, for example, an understood weakness in taking in verbally delivered instructions (number 3) is matched by an understanding of a strength in working independently from a book or worksheet (number 5). A realization that there is a danger of getting into trouble for shouting or hitting out (number 5) can be countered by the solution of remembering to use a taught anger-management technique (number 9). Clearly, since both lists will be highly individual to your child, not all problems and solutions will match as neatly, nor are all concerns going to be so easily addressed, but the technique is nonetheless useful. It gives both you and your child a chance to formalize what his difficulties are, what solutions he, you and the school have come up with so far that have worked, and what areas he has found in which he has confidence. This clear information will be invaluable as you begin the process of putting together information to pass onto the new school.

2.2 Sharing information about your child

Before going any further into how best to share this information, it is worth asking a question that may seem an odd one in the context of this book. Should you inform your child's new school about his AS diagnosis?

Your child has what is, to all intents and purposes, a 'hidden disability'. As such, the school staff need not know about your child's condition (at least at first) unless you inform them. It could be argued that he has the right to keep his medical condition confidential. Indeed, it is possible that you may not even have shared his diagnosis with him yet, so that he is unaware of it himself. Given these factors, disclosure about your child's AS automatically becomes a matter for consideration.

Without a shadow of a doubt I would recommend that your child be made aware of his own diagnosis, as a matter of right. It may be that you have not considered that he had the maturity to handle this up until now, but in the context of this move it is important to face up to this challenge during this transition period. If you fail to share your child's diagnosis with him now, you run the risk that he may pick up on parts of discussions and will hear the diagnosis by chance, or – worse – not hear it but simply come to the misguided conclusion that there is 'something wrong with him'. It is important to find a way to discuss your child's diagnosis with him and also, as is appropriate in your own family context and with his permission, with siblings and grandparents. Particularly important is to articulate not only the difficulties but also the strengths that his condition brings. There are a number of excellent books available on the best ways to share an autistic spectrum diagnosis with an individual, and indeed with the wider family, and now is an excellent time to address this issue (see Further Reading on p.157).

I would also recommend that the school be made aware of his diagnosis, as long as this is decided in agreement with your child. You cannot hope for your child to receive differentiated treatment to help with his AS if you do not share information about his condition with them. Within this recommendation, however, it may be more difficult to decide how widely to share the information. Should it just be shared with his teachers, or should you include non-teaching staff, other parents and other students? I think this decision should be based largely on your child's attitude to the diagnosis. If he is positive about it, it is likely he will share the information freely anyway, seeing (quite rightly) that there is nothing in it to be hidden. If he is less positive, you may have to be more subtle and require a more sensitive approach from the school. Some of your child's needs may be met successfully without disclosing the specific diagnosis to the wider school, and if this is your child's preference, his wishes will need to be respected. It is essential that you do some work with him on the whole issue of disclosure – talk to him about who he would be happy knowing his diagnosis, and about what he would like them and others to be told – and ensure that he is kept fully involved in all discussions. No one likes to feel they are being discussed 'behind their back', and it would be disrespectful to your child's increased maturity and adulthood to disclose anything that he would prefer to remain private. That said, the way he feels about his diagnosis is likely to have a great deal to do with how widely he is willing to have it disclosed, and if you have all been able to remain positive about AS it is more likely that he will see it as something to acknowledge and to work with – even to celebrate – rather than as something to hide.

Of course, sharing the diagnosis is only the very start. While it is essential that staff at his new school are aware of his AS diagnosis in order that they understand the need to differentiate for it, they need to be aware also of what your child is actually like. What frightens him? What makes him angry and how does he show it? What are his 'triggers'? Does he have academic difficulties, and if so what are they and how do they manifest themselves? What are his strengths and his skills? What are his interests? What has worked for him in managing his AS in school in the past? This is the information you have begun to gather, and you now have to decide how, and with whom, to share it.

What is an issue at this stage is whether you want to make a 'big thing' of your child's AS. It can feel that, if you make too much fuss, the diagnosis may be all that the new school will see, and they will fail to give your child a chance as an individual. On the other hand, if you are to have a chance to put into place the aids to transition recommended here, you are going to have to 'come clean'. You are not going to be able to have as open access as I recommend – the chance to take photographs, meet teachers, borrow books, make suggestions and generally get involved – unless you are clear about your child's AS. It may be tempting to play it down ('Really – he's fine. There's no need for any fuss…'), but that is not going to make the transition any easier. This is one of the occasions where over-emphasizing your child's needs may be more appropriate than under-emphasizing them. After all, in time the staff will get to know your child and will be able to make their own judgements. How much more likely is it that these will be favourable if, having had his needs met, they meet an assured, confident and 'successful' child from the start?

You will then need to decide on a format to share this information. What can be a good idea is to work with your child on a booklet, rather like an 'All About Me' project. This is a good way to involve your child and to include all the information you have gathered, and also to include many of the non-Asperger interests and characteristics that make your child unique. You could add this to the information being forwarded by his current school, and hope that together this information will begin to draw up a whole picture of your child. The named adult who is working with you and your child on transition should be ready to take on this information. You will need to discuss with her how she is going to share this information with your child's teachers.

Realistically, though, you need to be aware that most of your child's new teachers may be unlikely to become too familiar with the information forwarded by either your child's current school or by you. Although information about the children in their class is shared with each new teacher, it can be hard for them to take in when your child is only one of perhaps hundreds that the teacher is going to have to get to know. Indeed, it may even be difficult for teachers to identify your child using only a name or photograph. As well as the detailed information you would like to share as an ideal, therefore, you may decide that you also need a quick, 'easy access' way of sharing information immediately. For more details on this, see section 4.3.

2.3 Visiting the new school

One of the most successful strategies in your transition plan is likely to be visiting the school. The more you can enable your child to be familiar with the school environment, the better the transition to it is likely to be. The ideal for this is probably managing to visit the school, initially, when it is empty or at least very quiet. Going in at the end of the school day can be a great idea. The ideal is to allow your child to explore, to find his way from room to room, to become familiar with the smells of the Science labs and the echoing acoustic of the gymnasium, with the colours and ranges of the displays and (hugely important this), with the alarming and even painful issue of bells, whistles, sirens or the PA system. Arrange with the school that you let him read for a while in the library (it may have a far more comprehensive range of books around his interests than he is used to – or at least have new books he hasn't yet read), or perhaps allow him to use the school computers. If the school have an on-line library service, try to get him an access number now so that he can explore the database from home. Make sure that he has an opportunity to visit the bathrooms he is most likely to be expected to use. If your child is a girl it is essential you find out what the sanitary product disposal system is at the school, and make sure that she is familiar with the system. Do not assume that she will be able to generalize from a disposal system she has used previously: make sure she is clear on what to do in each of the various bathrooms around the school. If there are changing rooms or shower rooms, these also need to be explored. If you can find out where your child's locker is likely to be, see if he can find his way from it to his classroom base. Can he find the sports hall, the Art rooms, the Technology rooms? The more familiar your child can become with the actual school buildings themselves, before they are overwhelmingly filled by seething, noisy students, the better.

The next stage is to allow him to become familiar with the school with at least some students present. Can you go to an inter-school ball game in the gym? Does the school have an end of term review or play in the theatre? Many schools have Summer Fairs or Open Days aimed at prospective parents. You may well have attended these when choosing the school in the first place. Can you go back now, with your child, to get a further impression?

All of the above are activities that you should be able to take your child along to yourself, without too much additional permission from the school. When the school is either empty of students, or during an activity that allows parents and outside attendance, you may well be permitted to come into the school with few restrictions. When the school is full of students during the regular school day, however, there are likely to be much stricter restrictions in place. For your child to have plenty of access to the school during this time, which is after all how the school is going to be when he attends, it is most likely that he will need to be taken in by a member of support staff from his current school. This should be possible to arrange, and many schools are very happy to do so. It is time consuming, and it does involve 1:1 input from school staff, so it may be that it will not happen unless you request it, but it is a very reasonable request to make for a child with AS (indeed it is one it is reasonable to make over a number of occasions), so do feel confident when you do so.

It should be noted that this 'visiting the school' is to do with allowing your child to be familiar with the environment and to become more comfortable with the actual physical school itself. It may well be that there will be a number of other visits arranged, for your child, for you, for his current teachers, SENCO (Special Educational Needs Coordinator) and support workers in order to discuss your child, pass on information about him, present strategies that have worked for him in the past and so on. These meetings are in addition to the familiarization visits that I am proposing here. These are about the building, the environment and to a certain extent about the practicalities of content of school – curriculum books, lunch tickets and so on (see section 2.4 below). The others are more formal visits for or about your child. In the formal visits the attention is focused inward, on him; in the familiarization visits it is focused outwards, by him, towards the school. Both are important, but it is important to differentiate between them. There is unlikely to be time, during the more formal visits about your child, for you or for him to become sufficiently familiar with the school, nor to gather support materials (see section 2.4 below). Try to arrange the visits as separate entities with clearly defined separate purposes. That way, neither should impinge on the time of the other.

2.4 Collecting support materials

As well as physically allowing your child to become familiar with the school, and in tandem with these visits to familiarize him, there is plenty of support material you can collect to help him. With permission from the school, it should be possible to take photographs. Allowing your child to take a camera with him on his visits to look round the school can be a great idea. Photographs should not include individuals, especially students, without the school's written permission, but can include the physical environment, especially landmarks that your child can use to navigate his way around the site. The school should be able to supply you with a map of the site, and photographs and maps together should go a good way towards 'de-mystifying' the school and helping your child be confident that he will not get lost. These photographs can also be used to make communication aids, where, for example, a picture of the canteen is used as a visual prompt to remind your child where he has to go to get his lunch. Helpful, too, are photographs of the teachers your child is likely to encounter. You will need to get extra permission from the school to have these, but they should be available. Paste them in a notebook, with each photograph on its own page together with the teacher's name and subject and – if she has one – the location of her teaching room. This book will become even more useful as your child starts at the school as you begin together to make up a Teacher Book of different teacher traits and requirements (see section 4.4).

As your child visits the school prior to starting, try to be aware of, and if possible to begin to collect, the 'paraphernalia' of the school. This might include a pass card to open doors, a library card or computer access card, a locker key, lunch or other food tokens, late slips, attendance slips, permission to visit the bathroom passes, homework book, timetable and/or planner. If the school is willing to give you examples of these to take away with you, you can allow your child to become familiar with their use as well as coming up with practical ways of managing them (a key cord for the locker key, a wallet for the passes and so on). A copy of the timetable, even if only a blank, can be invaluable. Unfortunately, it may not be possible to have a copy of your child's real timetable before the beginning to the school year (timetables can change late in the school year due to staff changes, room changes and so on), but a blank, or perhaps last year's timetable, would give you a chance to help your child become familiar with the format. You can also help him to be familiar with the 'feel' of the day. Write up, perhaps on your shared transition plan, the times for registration, morning and afternoon teaching sessions, break and lunch times. Once these become familiar the underlying routine of the day at school will become much more secure. If the times given on the timetable are digital, now is the time to get your child a digital watch.

If they use the 24-hour format, make sure he understands that format now, before problems arise.

Equally useful, if the school is willing to let you borrow them, are some of the text books he will be using in different subjects. Familiarity with what he is going to be studying is likely to reduce his anxiety about it, and it is quite possible that these books will actually lead to enthusiasm for the whole 'new school' project. If your child with AS has a particular interest (our Sam has a particular passion for the sciences), having a text book packed with information about that subject can be very appealing. Text books are visual, and are packed with facts and information. They help the child with AS to focus on the curriculum aspect of the new school and away from the social, and as such are likely to be reassuring and attractive.

2.5 Identifying a named adult and 'safe haven'

When you begin to work with your child's future school you may have first contact with the Principal or Head Teacher, then perhaps be passed to a Head of Year or SENCO, a Transition Teaching Assistant (TA) or a Pupil Support Officer. While all of these people are going to be important in preparing a successful school environment for your child, it is important to find out fairly quickly who you should be dealing with on a day-to-day basis. When your child starts at the school he will need a named adult to whom he should go if he gets into difficulty. This named adult needs to be available (i.e. ideally not part time and therefore possibly not there, nor full-time teaching and therefore unable to be disturbed). You need to identify this named adult now, and begin working with her. She should be the person you go to in order to get permission to collect the support information mentioned above, as by doing so you are making her aware of what is being done to support your child now, and some ideas for what might work on into the future. She is the person who can get to know your child, understand his needs and vulnerabilities and appreciate his strengths and gifts. She will be the ideal person, if you can manage it, to come out to his current school and 'see him in situ', talk to his current teacher and support staff and understand what works for him currently and why. She might even be able to visit you and your child at home, and so get to know a little more about his home culture, his interests and what motivates him.

One thing to understand as you begin to put the process of smooth transition into action is about how schools work. A school year is seen very much as a unit. At the end of that unit, the top year group of the school take exams, then leave and move on and a new year group arrives at the bottom end. Teachers leave and new ones are recruited. Teachers who stay on are assigned different classes and the whole timetable alters. It can be very difficult, in this climate, to get anyone to really start thinking about the next academic year until this one has ended. Partly this is psychological. Teachers are tired at the end of the year, and are also extremely busy. They may have been working all year towards this point, to final exams, assessments, the end-of-year performance or whatever, and may not be ready to start thinking too much about what is going to happen after the summer break. It is also practical. Teachers and support staff may well not know which classes, year groups or even precise subjects they will be assigned the following year. Given this, it may be difficult to get the information on what it will be like when your child starts at the school, for example who his teachers will be, where his class base will be and so on, because the information may literally not yet be available. Although this may be frustrating when you want to get as much structure and reassurance in place as possible for your child, there may be nothing you can do about it. Rather than trying to take on the whole system (and run the risk of getting off to a bad start with your child's new school), you might do better to concentrate on the 'named adult' for your child. Once you have access to her, and if you are able to build up a positive relationship with her, she can be your bridge. It may even be possible, through her, to continue to receive information through the school holidays, as it becomes available. It should also be possible to disseminate information through her, so that you can be more confident that the teachers who 'get' your child next year, whoever they are, are prepared and knowledgeable.

Useful too to establish, as well as a 'named adult', is the safe haven to which your child will be able to go if confused or upset, as well as routinely during unstructured times such as break times and lunch. Ideally the two will be one and the same thing: the location to which your child should go will be where he finds his named adult. That is the ideal, but it may not be possible. It is necessary, therefore, to establish somewhere that is quiet, away from the bustle and clamour of the school, staffed (to prevent isolation and therefore the danger of bullying) and always accessible. Often this will be a learning support area, but it might be the library or a quiet study area. It might even, if the school are really AS-aware, be a dedicated room. Once you have established where the 'safe haven' is, make sure your child can find it from various points in the school. Use your after school visits to establish this room with your child as an attractive and secure place. If possible, use this room as your 'base' when your child visits the school. It is a great place to set up the familiarization meeting between your child and his named adult. If you establish right from the start that this is a safe haven there is much less chance of your child either running out of school or of finding somewhere less appropriate, and quite possibly less safe, for himself. However hard you try to make the transition smooth, the new school experience may well be very challenging and quite possibly overwhelming for your child with AS. Establishing where to go and who to turn to, should the situation become intolerable, is an essential step.

Important also is to establish how he will manage to access this safe haven. Will it be routinely available to him during unstructured times? Is it a place where other children with AS are encouraged to meet, thereby beginning the establishment of an AS community? Is it open to everyone or just to some people, and what are the rules of access? How can your child gain access to it in an emergency, when he begins to become overwhelmed? More details on how to manage granting your child access to the safe haven when needed are covered in section 4.8.

2.6 Identifying sensory difficulties and 'flagging them up' to the new school

The experience of feeling overwhelmed may be triggered, not by what anyone is doing to your child nor even by what he is being expected to do, but simply by the environment.

One of the points of allowing him plenty of access to the school buildings before he starts at the school is to allow him to become aware of strange smells, bright lights, loud noises. This sensory sensitivity in people with AS is something that is gradually becoming better understood. It may be that his brain is processing the information from his senses in a different way to that which the neuro-typical brain might do. For your child, sounds that seem almost inaudible to everyone else may be intensely distracting, even painful. The change of lesson siren or bell may be terrifying, and the anticipation of it, the fear that it may go off without warning, may be enough to prevent him managing the rest of the time at school. Similarly, some classrooms may be difficult for him because of their smell or because of pulsing fluorescent lights.

This sensitivity may be something that is difficult for the neuro-typical person to appreciate, and you may have to work hard to get sensitivities such as these taken seriously. The first step is going to be anticipating them, and you will already know what your child's problem areas might be. It is also well worthwhile shadowing him at his current school, and asking him which rooms he likes and, more importantly, which he doesn't like. He may never have thought to communicate to anyone that he hates sitting on the carpet in the classroom because of its scratchy texture or (like our Sam) that he particularly likes one room because of the 'soothing sound of the air conditioning unit'. Many of your child's quirks will need to be overcome, and most will probably be able to be managed with a little sensitivity and awareness. Understanding, though, will not happen unless you can describe his sensory processing eccentricities to the new school, so being fully aware of them yourself is a good first step.

2.7 Identifying useful technologies

As your child has grown up through his current school, it is likely that he will have come across specific difficulties which have impacted on his academic progress. Often these are quite mechanical. For example, it is not uncommon for children with conditions on the autistic spectrum to have motor or coordination difficulties, and this is often manifested in a problem with handwriting. Your child's writing may be untidy, slow, hard to read or even non-existent. It might be meticulous, with him unable to embrace the concept of 'rough work', drafting or note-taking. He may be unable to write any word he cannot immediately spell correctly. Whatever his individual quirks in writing or other academic areas, his teachers will have come up with strategies to help him to overcome them. The easiest of these to transfer successfully to his new school are the ones involving technology, especially if he can manage the technology for himself. It may be that for some time he has been using a word processor or computer when the other children in the class are handwriting, perhaps one available in class or even the teacher's own. If so, it is essential that you become aware of that now and begin the process where he takes over 'ownership' of the technology. This doesn't necessarily mean buying him his own lap-top, but it does mean establishing what technology he uses and how it is going to be made available when he moves school.

If he is using a computer, he needs to be confident with all stages of its use – turning it on, finding and saving files, printing out, transferring files, downloading information and so on. If the technology is to work for him, he will need to be able to 'manage' it, not have to rely on an adult to set it up for him. If you can show that he can manage the technology himself and that it will help rather than hinder his work across different subjects in his new school, you have a strong case for his being able to transfer with it to his new school. Technology is changing and developing on an almost daily basis, but the most advanced technology is not always going to be the most useful for him. A simple word processor or 'word harvester', designed for use in school may be more use than an expensive, top-of-the-range lap-top. For one thing, he is going to have to carry it around school, and avoid losing it, dropping it or having it stolen. If it is smaller, lighter, more robust and less enviable that might be to the better.

One of the biggest challenges your child is likely to face as he moves to a more senior school is that of staying organized. If he has different subjects across the day, in different locations and with different teachers he is going to have to be prepared with different books and equipment for each lesson and with recording the requirements of various types of homework. If he is having to manage technology different from his classmates, this may only add to confusion. If the teacher says she requires the students to fill in a worksheet, work in their books or 'make a sketch', how does this translate to the computer? I have known a 14-year-old with AS I was observing in school miss a whole lesson because the teacher began with the instruction to 'Divide your page in half.' The other students understood that this meant draw a line roughly down the middle of the page and then record the facts (they were on the physical differences between diurnal and nocturnal animals) in the appropriate section. The student with AS, who was using a lap-top, was thwarted by the instruction to divide the page. He didn't know how, on the programme he was using, to draw a line, nor how to create columns. His inability to carry out this first instruction meant that he failed to record the information about the animals that was being given by and to the other students, and would therefore have been unable to complete the assignment, which was being set for homework. The experience of observing this student taught me both how hard, and how easy, it is to accommodate many of the needs of the student with AS. It is hard because the teacher will often not anticipate where a student with AS may struggle. The teacher in this example had no idea that he was in difficulties and the student at no time asked for any clarification or help. It is easy because a problem like this is so easily solved (by the use of a prepared template divided into columns and with titles, for example…or, of course, by more accurate use of language by the teacher). There was no reason, in this example, to divide the page vertically; the work could just as easily have been completed as two separate lists on a blank page. If a prepared template had also included written instructions, including those for the completion of the assignment at home, then the problem would definitely have been avoided and the student would have been able to complete the task successfully.

The use of a computer or word processor can, therefore, be invaluable to the student with AS, but its use needs to be managed by the student himself and his teachers need to be aware that it is being used and accommodate for it. Technology can be a great support for people with AS, but it will never replace the need for understanding in those who work with them. Having said that, technology such as a palm-top computer or notebook can be invaluable, especially if it is a resource available to everyone involved with your child. Managed properly it can enable him to check where he should be, what he should be doing and when, and can carry specific information as needed to help alleviate anxiety. You can enter information into it including his timetable for each day, what he has to remember at each lesson, homework to be handed in and so on. His teachers can use it to record what is needed for homework assignments and by when they should be completed, and can use it as a quick communication tool between the school and home. It could be used to receive and send e-mails and texts, thereby allowing your child to stay in touch through the day with his named adult and with you and providing a way for him to seek clarification when he needs to. If you are considering using such a thing, now is the time to put it into use. Your child will need time to become familiar with it, to remember to use it and to develop ways that work best for him. If you practise now, while he is still in the relatively safe environment of a familiar school, you can develop its use ready for when he needs it after the move.

2.8 Identifying key skills to be developed (and habits to be broken) and working them into the transition plan

What you are doing by looking so closely on where your child is now in his current school, is looking to see what works (so that you can make sure these things continue), but also identifying the problems now, while there is still time to do something about them. These problems are likely to fall broadly into two categories: things he needs to learn to do, and things he needs to learn to stop doing.

The 'things he needs to learn to do' can be highlighted by going through his typical day and identifying where he is using extra support. It may be, of course, that he will continue to receive support in his new school, but at very least you will be identifying where that support is going to be needed to be put in place. More useful is identifying the areas where he continues to receive support but where, with a bit of extra input now, he could manage without. For example, has his teacher got into the habit of standing over him when they get changed for sports, turning his clothing the right way out for him and handing each item to him ready to be put on? If you think about it, you may realize that you do the same for him at home. What may be happening here is that your child is falling into a kind of 'learned helplessness', where he is used to receiving help, given because he is so slow, or else adults have got into the habit of doing things for him. If this is what is happening, it needs to stop. As he grows up, unless he becomes so wealthy that he can afford a personal servant, he is going to have to get dressed for himself. Withdraw the practical support now, and replace it with a system of rewards or motivators for getting changed within an allotted time. Step back and allow your child to take greater responsibility. His AS diagnosis hasn't changed, but he has grown up since last time you reviewed his need for help. You are not helping him if what you do does not increase, in the long run, his self-help and independence skills.

There may be any number of examples like this, both practical and academic, where your child has become used to receiving more help than he needs. On the other hand, there will be areas where he literally lacks the necessary skills to manage independently. These may be quite practical life skills like, for example, being able to read and calculate time, or being able to count or to understand money. Some of these may be absolutely essential (for example, being able to cross the road safely). He is likely to need more support with some of these skills than his neuro-typical peers, and if you can realize that they are a weakness now, support for improving his skill in them can be written into his transition plan and time can be put aside for helping him, even in the school day. Identifying these missing skills now, while there is still time to do something about them, is one of the most powerful arguments for having a '2-year plan' ahead of moving schools.

Perhaps his lack of skill is more abstract. Perhaps you might become aware that he needs extra support learning how to queue, to take turns, to ask for help, to make decisions. Now, while he is in a safe and known environment, is the time to get him some extra input with these life skills. The more 'able' he can become in these areas, before he faces the challenge of a whole new and strange environment, the better.

The other side to this 'skills base' is to identify what he needs to learn to stop doing. His change of school will, almost definitely, lead him into a more adult environment than his current one, and habits that have been tolerated by his peers up until now may very well not be tolerated at his new school. The obvious, of these, are the 'baby habits', for example sucking his thumb, fingers or jumper, or needing to carry a comfort object or toy or wear a particular item of clothing. It is tempting, in your fear for how he will be accepted at 'big school', to forcibly remove his comfort items, and to deal punitively with what you see as babyish habits of suckling or mouthing. In fact, before you do so, you need to remind yourself that your child has AS.

Mouthing or sucking can be highly comforting, and indeed may even be palliative. There may even be some pressure points in the mouth which, if pushed, help relieve pain. If your child with AS is constantly pushing his fingers into his mouth it may be worth checking that he does not do so because it relieves pain, for example from a headache due to uncorrected vision, or from an ear infection or tooth abscess. Even if his reason is not so concrete, there will be a reason why he sucks or chews at hands or clothing, even if that reason is only that it reduces stress, or just that he finds it pleasurable. A talisman object or 'lucky' item of clothing are also ways of bringing order to a confusing world. For the child with AS, there is very little about his environment or his day over which he has control. Wearing a certain pair of socks or carrying a special stone in his pocket may give him an impression of almost magical protection. To take this magic away without consultation, or to punish behaviours that are helping your child to cope, would show a lack of sensitivity or kindness that would leave your child even more isolated and vulnerable.

Your problem is that, although you may understand his need to carry his small square of rag or to chew at the cuff of his coat, you know also that these behaviours leave him open to ridicule and rejection by his peers. It can be very hard to reconcile these two positions as the parent of a child with AS.

The reason you are tackling these behaviours now is that you have plenty of time to take things slowly. Because you are doing so now, when the situation is stable, they may be safely resolved by the time you add in the increased stress of the new school. Look at your child's behaviours, and first work out which ones need to be eliminated, and which can be adapted. If it is a piece of cloth that your child needs to carry, could this be sewn inside a pocket? If it is a lucky stone, could you have that made into a key ring? (Be aware that you should only do these with your child's full knowledge as either of these could, potentially, destroy the worth of the object in his eyes.) If your child has a particular interest, check out what merchandise is available. It may be possible that they already make objects for school use, e.g. erasers, pencil toppers, key fobs, etc. that you could introduce now to allow time for them to become important to him. What is important is that you take plenty of time and treat the situation sensitively. Your child is using these habits as coping strategies, and you need to work with him on introducing alternative, more acceptable strategies as well as understanding, and helping to manage, the sources of the stress.

2.9 Encouraging the 'named adult' to visit the current school

It may be that you have difficulty identifying these areas, both the skills that need to be developed and the habits that should be broken. This is partly because children grow up very gradually, for us who are with them every day, and it can be difficult to step back and see our own child clearly. We get used to having the nine-year-old, yet before we know it he has turned ten! It's also true that we are unlikely to be aware of the precise skills needed at the next school, nor perhaps even aware of how little tolerated certain habits might be. For this reason, and for others, it is hugely helpful if the child's 'named adult' can come in and visit the child in his current school.

This visit gives the opportunity for the 'named adult' to see the child in a school setting, and to see him relaxed. There are two, rather separate, sets of difficulties with moving school. One set is to do with how the child will manage the issue of change itself, and the other to do with how he will manage at the new school. This visit allows the support worker from the new school to assess the latter, free from the stresses of the former. When he starts at the new school, the very fact of it being new and different is likely to be the over-riding influence. This visit to assess the child in a stable, familiar setting gives a much fairer indication of how he will cope after the 'change' element has been managed, and also to give suggestions of skills needed and habits to be broken.

These habits may be fairly mundane. For example, many primary and elementary schools encourage students to write using pencil, yet most middle, secondary and high schools require use of ink. This change is absorbed by most neuro-typical children so seamlessly that they could not tell you when they switched from one medium to the other. For some children with AS, however, this change is so fundamental that it may lead to loss of almost all writing skills. For the child with AS, writing with a pen is simply not the same as writing with a pencil.

The visiting teacher should be able to identify these differences without difficulty, as long as she is AS-aware enough to know to do so. She will need to be sensitive to quite subtle differences in ways the day-to-day management of learning and teaching is delivered. Does the new school use A4 writing sheets rather than exercise books? Is the outside space called a 'yard' rather than a 'playground'? Will Computer Time soon be called ICT and Technology called D&T? What about the correct way to address the teacher? Is there a switch from using the teacher's name to calling male teachers 'Sir' and female teachers 'Miss'? These differences will be so many, and so difficult to predict (they will vary between school and school in the same small town; it is a certainty they will vary between state and state, country and country and continent and continent). The problem may be that the visiting teacher or support worker may not be sufficiently familiar with AS to be aware that she needs to identify these differences. You may have to find other ways to gather the information.

One of the most efficient ways to identify, to list, these differences at even the most 'tiny' level (which may well be far from 'tiny' to the person with AS) is to ask a student, preferably one who has AS himself. If a student with AS can be supported to visit your child's current school and be given the specific task of identifying all the differences in language and in educational practice (don't let him get started on the physical differences between the buildings or you'll be there all day!), it is likely that he would do a superb job. Later, when you give feedback to the schools on ways to help improve transition for students with AS, this may be something you can suggest. You may even volunteer to allow your child to take on the mission. For now, it is an ideal that may be difficult to organize – but which remains an ideal.

You may, of course, be lucky enough to have a visiting teacher or support worker who is fully AS-sensitive. If so, she will be able to pick up on many of the differences, and be able to help identify areas on which to work with your child before the transition takes place. This visit is also an excellent opportunity for her to access the expertise of your child's current teachers and support staff. No amount of paperwork and reports will be as effective as open, respectful exchange between professionals, and if that can be facilitated it must be to the good. This is an opportunity for the new school's teacher to see supports that are working for your child in action. It is a chance to witness your child as a 'successful' school student, and to establish a level of attainment to be maintained, once the difficulties of transition itself have been overcome. It is a chance for the representative of the new school to 'pick the brains' of all those who have made school work for your child so far. It is also a great chance to get to know your child on his own, familiar, ground. Your child is much more likely to begin to establish a relationship and a level of trust with this new 'named adult' if he can accept her as means of transition – as someone who spans both environments.

This visit also gives the visiting teacher the opportunity to introduce elements of the new school into the old. These may be practical (perhaps a diary or an organizer, a certain calculator or a specific dictionary or thesaurus) or they may be more abstract. Perhaps she may identify that the child is in the habit of approaching the teacher and getting her attention by tapping her arm. The visitor may be aware of how unacceptable this will be at the new school, and can ask the child's current teacher to begin establishing a more acceptable way of gaining attention (putting up the hand, saying excuse me, etc.) during the remaining weeks at the current school.

One of the elements that becomes apparent when discussing transition between schools, for all pupils, is how little the majority of the teachers and staff working at each level of establishment understand what happens in the other. Perhaps individual members of staff, tasked with working on transition, might make the journey across to the other establishment, but the majority of staff are too busy managing the day-to-day demands of their own students to be able to go 'visiting'. In many ways this is a shame, as it leaves the students to manage the transition for themselves, and for some, particularly in this case for those with AS, this is something they do indeed struggle to manage. Worryingly, the adults on whom they have come to rely may genuinely not know the answer to concerns that are preoccupying the child, and this lack of expertise may further alarm the vulnerable child. Nor do parents, routinely, know much about the actual hour-to-hour workings of most schools. It is not surprising, in this context, that rumours originating from the students themselves are rife and very potent.

Part of the job of facilitating transition for the child with AS is to reassure him that there are adults in charge, and that these adults do possess the necessary expertise. The transition plan, already mentioned, is vital in this as it identifies not only *what* is to be done, but also *by whom*. It identifies, in other words, who the adults in charge of each part of the transition are, and who are the experts. It can be immensely reassuring to know who is piloting the ship, and if you know he really does know how to navigate by the stars, then that is all the better!

2.10 Working out a 'transition time-line' with clear identification of responsibilities for all involved

Your transition plan, first mentioned in Chapter 1, will by now be becoming more detailed. This is the 'life-belt' document that is going to support your child through this move. It began life as something very simple, perhaps as simple as 'Leave School A (date) and Start at School B (date). By now it will have a great deal of detail added to it. You will have added the times of each of the visits you have made to the school, made a note of the names of who you saw, and written in the time and date for the named adult to come in to your child's current school. As such, it has been a practical diary document, giving some logic and structure to the process of the approaching move. Now, though, it begins to be so much more.

It is important that the plan incorporates, in some preferably visual form, a projection into the future. It is important for you and your child to be able to see what is going to be happening, and to have a concept of when. It is during this time, incidentally, that you are going to have to make some decisions about just when 'Leave School A' and 'Begin School B' are going to be, as discussed later in sections 3.1 and 4.1. What was a simple document recording the seemingly inevitable, is now becoming something far more organic, something that can be used to make decisions and which can incorporate change and flexibility as decisions are made. Much of what is added to the plan from now on needs to be reactive to your child's direction and concerns.

It is helpful if the plan has somewhere to record questions, as they occur. Perhaps you could get into the habit of encouraging your child to jot down questions on a board as they occur to him, and for you to do the same. For each question, add a response indicating how you are going to go about answering it, when it will be addressed, who you will ask. As this process takes place, record it visually on the plan. This ability to ask questions, and to see those questions resolved into answers, with a transparency to the process of how the answers were reached, can be tremendously reassuring.

Of course, this process is most effective if you can get clear answers, and for this reason it does no harm to jot down some fairly 'answerable' questions yourself to get the process going. For example, you might ask, one morning, if your child knows what time the new school day starts and finishes. If he doesn't, jot down the thought as a question on the board. Add to it when you are going to find out, and how. For example, you might add an arrow to a notice 'Look it up tonight' with another saying 'Look on school website.' When the answers have been found, add them to the board. This may seem rather mechanical and contrived, but by doing this you are opening up a means of dialogue for your child's concerns. One of the challenges of dealing with a child with AS is to facilitate communication. He may not think to articulate something that is worrying him if he does not think you have the answer. The transition plan board throws open the concept that it is okay to ask questions, and that together you can seek out answers. It gives recurring sources of answers ('look on the web', 'consult the prospectus', 'ask the named adult', etc.), and it gives your child some control over what and when the 'next move' in the transition process might be. By flagging up approaching visits to the school, and identifying these visits as ways of getting answers to questions, you are again empowering your child to become involved in his transition process. Above all, you are encouraging him to question, seek solutions and have a forum to express concerns. Not all answers may be as easy to address as the simple ones given above, but most will involve very similar channels to address them. You are establishing a way for your child to indicate his concerns and fears, and are treating these as rational, practical problems. The firmer established this line of communication can be before you really get into the 'thick' of the move, the better.

2.11 Dealing with rumours

One of the biggest problems with the perceived concept that there are no answers to his concerns (and that the adults around him do not have sufficient knowledge or expertise to answer these concerns) is that your child will be very vulnerable to rumour. Rumours, usually originated by the older child who has already been through the 'ordeal' of moving up, and frequently spread by younger siblings fearful of what their older siblings have told them, are usually rife around the subject of moving schools. These rumours are particularity prevalent around the issue of bullying (particularly around the issue of initiation into the ways of the new school) and around the viciousness and unreasonableness of certain teachers. According to child lore, all new children get their lunch money stolen, their heads flushed down the pan and are kept behind by bawling teachers the first time books are forgotten or work not completed on time.

These rumours are alarming to all children, but the neuro-typical child has the defence of having at least some concept of 'taking them with a pinch of salt'. For the child with AS, his tendency to take things literally may make him far more vulnerable, and indeed, his very awareness that he is 'different' may make him aware that he does in reality face more dangers than his socially-adept neuro-typical peers. The child with AS is both more vulnerable to the fear of bullying, and historically more vulnerable to actual incidents of bullying. He may well fall foul of teaching staff who do not understand his condition. Anxiety around these subjects needs to be taken very seriously indeed.

The first thing to do is to try to counter the effectiveness of the rumours. Statistics and hard-bitten facts may help hugely. If you can find documented evidence that no pupil has been killed at the school, only one has been hospitalized (for a sporting injury) and that no one has been charged with assault in the past X number of years, this may help. It needs to be emphasized that bullying is another name for intimidation and assault, and that the law exists to protect against these things in school in just the same way as in outside society. If lunch money really is being stolen, this is theft and is a criminal offence to be dealt with as such. If heads really are being held in toilet bowls this is assault, and the same is true. Try to explain to your child that the rule of law exists in school just as in the rest of society. These rumours or urban myths exist, and have always existed, and are usually without any basis in truth.

It is important to bear in mind just how potent these fears can be. If you as an adult had to enter a working environment every day where you had real fear of actual violence, your quality of life would be very poor. Your ability to do a good job would certainly be jeopardized and it is unlikely you would be in a position to learn very much. As an adult it is important that you make the judgement about how realistic fears of bullying might be. It is a sad but inescapable fact that for some children, in some schools, the threat is not exaggerated. Children are, sometimes, attacked in school, and some very occasionally are even killed. Before you can even begin to deal with the anxiety of your child with AS, you need to quantify, realistically, how justified that anxiety is. It is no good telling your child he is safe if he is not.

However, it is also extremely important, if you are confident that your child *is* safe, to find a way of effectively communicating this fact to him. Your child's level of fear about bullying may in no way correlate to his real level of danger. While it is essential you take his fear seriously and do not underestimate its power, it is also important that you help him to keep it within manageable bounds. The fear of bullying may be deeply incapacitating in itself.

The other traditional focus for rumour around this time is around the viciousness and unreasonableness of teachers. Your child will probably hear how strict teachers are, how unreasonable, how hasty to deal out punishments and sanctions. Again, you need to counter these rumours with fact. I have heard one child attempt to reassure another that teachers are not allowed to bite or kick you at middle school 'without a good reason'! We may find this amusing, but by definition children's fears are childish. Reassure your child that the school discipline code works both ways and that rules about treating each other with respect, being polite and so on work as much from the teachers to the pupils as vice versa. Teachers at middle, secondary and high school are still that: teachers. On the whole they are to be trusted.

One final point, though. With the issue of bullying perhaps what your child with AS needs to hear more than anything else is that you are taking his concerns seriously, that you accept that it is possible, and that you will not allow it. While he is still a child, he has reduced autonomy and he relies on you to protect him. You may need to reiterate that that protection is there. Give him absolutes. Assure him that if anyone were to attack him, you would respond, and that you would and will take responsibility for resolving the problem. Reassure him that bullying will not be tolerated, not just by the school but by you. Although it is heartily to be hoped that you will not have to use it, the promise that if the problem is not resolved *he will not have to go to the school* may well be the single element that makes transition to the school successful. I would even put it up on the transition plan. 'You will not have to go into "X" school if you are being hurt' may sound extreme, but perhaps, in its simplicity, it is a commitment that you need to articulate. Such a simple statement may help you both to be clear that your child's safety is paramount, and that you can guarantee it. One of the worst sicknesses of the bullied child is the belief that no one can do anything to stop the bullying. Bullying may go unreported because, as the bully will say, 'they' (i.e. adults) can do nothing to help. Sometimes only a promise as simple and as radical as that you will not make your child go into a dangerous environment is potent enough to combat the fear that rumours can create. As such, it is worth making – and meaning.

2.12 Adapting current strategies that work for supporting transition

In many ways, although this transition between schools feels so huge, it is only another example of something that your child may already have difficulty with – and which you have therefore developed strategies for solving. Many children with AS find routines reassuring and change difficult to handle. Because of that, we who live with them and those who work with them will have developed techniques that can now be adapted to meet this bigger challenge. So, for example, you may have the habit of giving your child a 'five minute warning' before a change in activity. Certainly, five minutes set on a timer to explain that the computer game is going to be turned off leads to a great deal less stress than if you just turn the machine off without warning. Taking that technique, your transition plan is very much the same thing. You are giving warning that this change is approaching, and are giving a visual indication of when, and of what is going to happen during that change. Many children with an autistic spectrum disorder (ASD) find that having an object helps them in transition. So, for example, to get a young child with an ASD to come in from playtime back to the classroom, a teacher might have developed the technique of giving the child a car from the toy car mat, which the child then knows means that he makes his way in to the mat and has some minutes playing. Similarly, in our situation, allowing the pupil to become familiar with new text books eases the transition into that lesson, giving familiarity with lunch tokens and the lunch routine eases transition to that. Buying your child his 'new' school bag and letting him get used to it at his old school, buying and 'breaking in' new clothing and shoes, sports equipment and stationery can all help soften the transition barrier.

When you have become familiar enough with the routines and expectations of your child's new school, you are in a position to prepare many visual prompts to help him manage his new day. Most schools provide a planner and timetable – both a great start for the child with AS. See section 4.1 for many ideas on ways to use familiar techniques to support your child once he has started at the school.

2.13 Utilizing existing AS community of the school

One of the tips that is routinely given to neuro-typical pupils making a change of school is to get to know someone from the same year group. While this person may never develop into a friend, it can be hugely reassuring for many pupils to have someone to arrive with, someone to 'hang out' with until they become more confident.

Although this attitude may be true for some children with AS, for many it will seem an irrelevance. This sort of 'social supporting' does not come naturally to the individual with AS, and it is unlikely that an individual with AS would see that merely having someone else with them who is also lost and new is going to help at all. On the other hand, there is still potential for support to be offered from this sort of source, especially if the school already has an established AS community.

With the number of cases of ASD occurring now estimated in at least 1 per cent of the population, there are highly likely to be other students with AS at the school. Whether they are 'visible' to you will depend greatly on the school's ethos. They may be an invisible group with no sense of identity, or they may have come together to form what can only be described as an Asperger community. If a safe haven is available to students with AS in a school, and is being used at break and lunch times, the students who go there may find that they share similar interests. What may happen is that from these interests, small 'sub-clubs' develop, where students swap their card collections, build Lego creatures, play chess or computer games together...or whatever. These 'sub-clubs' may not, primarily, be socially motivated, but nevertheless they do provide a community where the individual with AS feels accepted and at home.

If this sort of Asperger community has been encouraged to develop at the new school, it can be a tremendous source of support for your child. Here is a point in the day where he is likely to feel at home, be able to avoid stress and recharge, and where he can feel accepted. Managed properly, the community can give excellent practical support and advice. Older students with AS can provide AS-appropriate explanations to younger students which may be eye-openers to their neuro-typical support staff, and can be a wonderful source of AS-useful information about the school. Additionally, the community can provide support and reassurance for parents (as current parents will have been through many of the issues concerning new parents and can reassure, pre-empt or explain) and a vehicle for AS-specific education. Much time is spent in a traditional timetable on 'life skills'-type subjects – community, sex and drugs education, study skills, relationship counselling, self-knowledge and so on. Much of this, as delivered traditionally, will not be particularly appropriate to the pupil with AS. If an AS community has been allowed to develop, there is encouraging potential to allow time for AS experts to visit the school and to explore these and other issues with the students in an AS-appropriate way.

Of course, all students with AS are different, and there is no particular reason why individuals with AS should get on better with each other than with anyone else. Indeed, the lack of social sensitivity may, in fact, double the problem. On the other hand, it is quite possible that the lack of emphasis on social interaction may mean that students with AS will indeed find that they enjoy each other's company, and this 'similarity' may be sufficient to overcome other barriers of behaviours or age.

For the child visiting the school prior to moving, this community could provide the perfect introduction. Asking an older student with AS to show your child around may mean that your child gets a perspective on the school that is far more appropriate. Asking the older student to come up with 'Three Top Tips' to making a successful start could result in some valuable advice. For you, talking to another parent who has a child with AS could well give you both reassurance and prior warning of potential pitfalls ahead.

Asking for the chance to do these things will also give you a useful clue as to the way that the school views AS. If it is difficult because you are told that 'it would be breaking confidentiality' to tell you of other students with AS then there is a good chance that the school sees AS as something negative, and to be kept hidden. If an older student with AS is only too proud to tell you about the ways he and the school have managed and accommodated his AS, this is a healthy sign that your child, in turn, will be valued and integrated.

2.14 Familiarizing your child with the school, and with the concept of the school

One of the easiest ways to aid transition, once you are sure of where your child is going, is the 'drip effect'. Find as many ways as possible to familiarize your child with the school. Look for references to sports fixtures, drama performances and so on in your local press. Begin to follow the school teams, even if only through checking the results of fixtures, and look out for posters and reviews of performances. Find excuses to drive or walk past the school, spot students as they catch buses or trains around your town and do everything you can to mention the school often and in the best possible light. Get into the habit of referring to the school into the future ('Next summer, when you are on vacation from X, perhaps we can go sailing...' and so on).

In a sense, what your child is going to have to do is 'redraw' himself in his own mind as a member of the new school as opposed to a member of the old. Many individuals with AS find this concept of 'belonging' quite hard to grasp, and it may have taken some considerable time for your child to have fully accepted loyalty to his current school. He is likely to find it harder than his neuro-typical peers to switch that loyalty and belonging, now, to a new school. The sooner you can begin this integration process, where he can come to terms with the idea that he is a member of this new institution and that his identity is, in a sense, tied up with that, the better. The society of a school is nearly always sufficiently strong that it extends its protection and 'belonging' to all its members, even if within that society finding a way of fitting in may be more difficult. In other words, although your child may find getting himself fully included into the various cliques and sets within a school a considerable challenge, inclusion in the overall membership is just about guaranteed. Cheering for the school when it is competing against another school is seldom likely to be 'wrong'.

3

The Holidays

3.1 Looking at strategies to minimize distress at leaving the old school

As careful as you try to be, leaving the old school may be distressing for your child with Asperger syndrome (AS). Much of his security, familiarity and routine is likely to be tied up in the place and the people, and he may feel very insecure to be leaving these behind. While for the neuro-typical child there is considerable comfort in promises to 'keep in touch' from individuals, for the child with AS these may be no help at all. He may feel no desire at all to maintain social contact with his peers, and even if he does, may not see this as relevant to the current situation. What he may be distressed about is the loss of 'sameness' and predictability. The possibility that he might see some of these people again somewhere else is unlikely to compensate for the fact that he is losing this place, these smells, these sounds, the knowledge of where to go, what to do and how to act.

In addition, this security is likely to be undermined in the lead up to leaving the school. For many pupils with AS, the last days and weeks of any school term or year can be a difficult time. Routines change, rules are relaxed, quiet individual work tends to be replaced by group and social activities and there can be an increase in 'secret' activities (for example, collections made for teachers who are leaving, secret rehearsals for end of term songs to be sprung on unsuspecting staff, etc.). Often the timetable itself can be altered during the last weeks of term as teachers take days out to visit their new jobs, and existing children move around to experience their new classrooms. Visits are made by the new pupils to the school, and, of course, days are arranged for the students to visit their new schools.

Quite often, parents are left at the beginning of the holidays in despair as their child's behaviour becomes erratic or withdrawn. What has, up to then, been a successful term or year, finishes with everyone from parents and teachers to the child himself losing confidence and feeling that school is not going as well as it might. This feeling, and this phenomenon, is only likely to be more pronounced at the upheaval of actually leaving the school.

The actual last day of school can be even more difficult. Many people (pupils and parents, and sometimes even teachers) cry. This overflowing of emotion is probably quite enjoyable for many, or at least is cathartic, but for the child with AS it may be traumatic. He may not understand this increase in emotion, and may even find it frightening. In addition, conventional barriers are broken down, particularly barriers of personal space. Everyone may start to hug everyone else! For the individual with AS, who may have very set barriers around his personal space and who may have worked hard at managing and understanding conventional rules of space and physicality, this sudden loss of rules may be disorientating and alarming. He may not want to be hugged.

Given that the onset of this 'chaos' is predictable, it may be worth considering an early exit from school. If, for example, your child left a week early this would give him a chance to make a distinct break, but in an ordered way. If he is the only child going round getting his year book signed, this can lead to an appropriate level of seriousness and attention to the fact that he is leaving, but at the same time to a calm and measured approach. It may be that he is singled out for a separate 'goodbye' in assembly, but in a way that is suitable to him and to his style. This personalized, differentiated exit can be managed to be far more meaningful, and far less traumatic than continuing to the general exodus of the last day.

An early exit has the added value of giving you an 'extra week' while schools are likely still to be open, which gives valuable extra opportunity for visits to the new school. However, it is worth bearing in mind that these schools will also be in the 'chaos' of the end of the year, and may not be as calm and reassuring as you might hope. Perhaps more important with an early exit is that it gives an extra week's holiday, before other schools have broken up. This quiet extra week, perhaps when siblings are still at school, or when museums, attractions and galleries are still relatively empty, can give a great opportunity for your child to have a rest, a quiet week of stillness to begin to absorb some of the changes that are coming to him. The early finish is certainly something worth thinking about.

Another option, one which is particularly attractive when twinned with a flexi-start (see section 4.1), is a flexi-finish. This means only sending your child into school for shorter periods during the last few weeks, while getting him used to the idea that he works for the remaining time independently at home. He might cope better with the end of term performance if he has had the morning away from school, or with the sports day if he knows he goes home immediately after it. This strategy works well, again, with making visits into the new school as it further blurs the edges and makes his schooling more of a continuous event. There is more on making a 'flexi-start' in Chapter 4.

3.2 Providing preparation and support during the holiday period

One of the challenges you face, however well you manage your child's exit from his current school, is to maintain the calm and the momentum during the holidays. You are faced with an unstructured time when your child (typically) gets out of the routines of school and loses much of the stability that reliance on those routines can bring. In this case, with no safe resumption of those routines on the horizon, your child may suffer considerable anxiety.

Continued reliance on your transition plan can help enormously. Write into the plan dates and times to go shopping for school shoes, sports kit, pens and pencils, etc., spacing these activities over several occasions. If possible, continue to visit the school. The office, if nothing else, is likely to remain open for much of the holiday, and this is an opportunity to call in, even if only to make an enquiry or to pick up a sports-clothing list. If it can be arranged, further opportunities to explore the now empty school can be of huge benefit, especially as now that the academic year has ended it should be possible to be told where your child's home base room will be, and even to pick up a copy of his timetable. Rooms are often repainted during the summer break, so now is a chance to get an idea of the school as it will be when your child starts.

One technique that may help your child with AS is to spend part of the holidays acclimatizing him to the rhythms of his new day. If you can bear it during vacation time, get into the habit of getting up at the time he will have to for school, having breakfast at the correct time, being ready to leave the house at the time he will have to. Have lunch during the time in the day when it will available to him when he is at school, and get him used to the procedures he will be using (see section 3.3). If you can get your child used to the rhythms of the day he will be using, whether this is when he gets up, eats, or when he visits the bathroom, it will make the transition into this rhythm at school a great deal easier.

In a similar way, building familiarity with school clothing and footwear will help too. If the school has a uniform it may not be practical to wear it all during the holidays, but there is nothing to stop your child from getting used to wearing, for example, the trousers with his usual casual top, or the shirt under his sweatshirt. Some clothing can cause skin irritation or other discomfort to people with AS, who may be more sensitive to differences in textures, the presence of labels or to unfamiliar restriction than is usual. It may be that the school requires boys to wear a tie, or for girls to wear tights rather than socks. If so, the holiday is an ideal time for your child with AS to become familiar with this sensation. Build up the wearing of new clothing gradually, and use this time to see if strategies such as removing labels or replacing buttons with hooks-and-eyes may help.

Similarly, the school may have different expectations for sportswear than those with which you are familiar. Allow plenty of opportunity for your child to change in to and out of sports kit and shoes. He needs to learn how to lace boots now, not find himself unable to do so when he is about to go onto the field. Wearing items such as helmets, shin-guards and mouth shields may be difficult and even alarming for some individuals with AS. Again, gradual exposure in a non-threatening environment is far more likely to lead to success than sudden exposure in an already demanding situation.

3.3 Addressing practical issues

Although it doesn't necessarily make for much of a 'holiday', this period of transition can be invaluable if you use it to address many of the challenges your child with AS will be facing at his new school. Indeed, it may be best to commit yourself to a period of intensive preparation. Have the 'holiday' first, but then give over the final couple of weeks to a programme of preparation. It is an investment of time that will be well worthwhile.

Your programme will vary, depending on the needs of your individual child. For example, one of the new stresses facing your child might be catching a bus in the mornings where before he used to walk or be dropped off at school by you. Your child with AS may be anxious about this (although he may not say so unless directly prompted), but what may not be clear is what it is about the experience that is making him anxious. Is it the possibility of missing the bus? Is it the issue of where to sit, how to get a ticket or how to use a pass, or is it the fear of being squashed in a crowd? Perhaps it is anxiety about catching the wrong bus and the fear of being carried off the route and of getting lost? Anxiety about an issue such as catching buses can be alleviated if you spend the time now making this a known and accepted activity. Catch buses together. Drop your child at a bus stop and arrange to meet up with him again at the station. If possible, arrange for your child to make the route from your house to the school a number of times – and to make the route home again. Increase confidence around independent travel generally. You might make a quite ambitious journey, across the country or indeed into a foreign country, encouraging your child to read the timetables, make the decisions, buy the tickets. Let him choose where to sit on the bus, and get him used to standing in a busy, jostling crowd. If you can build success at a *more* stressful level than that he will experience on the way to school, it will build increased confidence about facing this daily activity.

Similarly, your child with AS may face a canteen system for the first time at his new school. Choosing what to eat (indeed, making choices generally) may be challenging for him, as may eating using institutional crockery and cutlery (which may be considered unhygienic) or eating at tables that have been wiped by a 'dirty' cloth or which have crumbs or other people's used plates or food stains on them. The whole business of lunch – queuing for food, deciding what to get, deciding where to sit, eating in front of others or watching others eat – may be a source of anxiety for an individual with AS. As with the buses, now is a great opportunity to support your child in overcoming these anxieties. Eat out! Practice using a variety of restaurants and canteens, working towards encouraging your child to queue alone, make his choices independently and pay for himself. Be there to support him through each stage, but keep on encouraging greater and greater independence. Incidentally, make sure that this support extends to using as wide a variety of bathrooms as is possible too. All sanitary equipment is not the same. Some places have urinals, some have cubicles. Women's bathrooms have a wide range of sanitary disposal arrangements. Some facilities are clean and some, frankly, are dirty. It may be that the facilities at school are not of the standard you would prefer, but your child with AS still needs to be able to use them. Visit some really disgusting ones and work out a strategy to manage. Approach the problem together in a calm and logical way. Would a tube of 'dry' disinfectant hand-wash, as used in hospitals, help to alleviate anxiety?

Some of the skills you will need to encourage and to develop are quite amorphous. They include things like 'being organized' and 'being able to get help'. You could start to develop using a check-list, for example to pack to go camping, and see if this helps. More simply, you could try it for daily chores at home. Has your child washed/ brushed his teeth/fed the rabbit/tidied his room? Check-lists to manage and impose order and routine can be a great source of security for some individuals with AS, and if you have the technique 'up and running', it is more readily available for when it is needed for school. Many people find addressing strangers and asking for assistance daunting. Practice in more secure environments (asking for a certain book at the library, buying a ticket at the train station) before facing the more challenging ones such as asking directions in the street. Practise together on practical skills such as reading a map and decoding a timetable. Keep all of this light-hearted and as fun as possible. Make it into a game and keep the emphasis always on achievement. Keep on reiterating what your child *can* do, and try to restrict *can't do* to setting achievable targets and challenges. For example you could try something like, 'I bet you can't find out the ISBN number on the book "X" quicker than I can check out this book "Y" – the winner chooses the ice cream!' This could involve all kinds of interaction, asking, using computers and problem solving – and choosing the flavour and asking for the ice cream are moves towards independence too.

Bear in mind, however, that greater independence leads to greater vulnerability, and it is essential that you give your child with AS the tools now that will keep him safe. Ensure that he is secure about safe procedures such as those for crossing roads, and make sure that he has plenty of practice across as wide a range as possible of environments. Try to challenge him to come up with solutions should situations change. What would he do if traffic lights were broken? What would he do if roadworks barred his usual path? Even more challenging, but just as important, you will need to go through what is appropriate and inappropriate behaviour, and make sure that he is absolutely sure about both what is an inappropriate advance and what to do about it. Be very specific about what parts of the body other people are allowed to touch. Individuals with AS may be particularly vulnerable to sexual assault, and you need to be confident now that you are giving your child strategies to deal with this situation in case it should arise, and to tell you if it does. The strategy, 'Alert others and move to safety', is one simple one; coach your child in a loud, 'Stop touching me!' and in moving away towards a safe group of people. Important also is that he is aware of personal space. Knowing not to stare at another person on a bus or train, not to make personal comments, not to stroke someone's top however soft and appealing the texture…all are details the independent traveller with AS will need to learn. He is also going to have to learn when not to make personal comments about people, and when not to get into conversation. Social naivety can make him very vulnerable, as not everyone takes kindly to a youth telling them that the notice says not to put their feet up on the seat, or that it is against the law to be smoking on the train. Travelling and being 'out and about' with your child with AS during this holiday period will probably give you plenty of opportunities to observe and to advise on specific situations. Be aware, though, that he may find generalizing what you say from one situation to another difficult, and may make similar 'mistakes' again and again. At very least, your holiday time together may make you aware that, actually, he is not yet ready to catch the bus alone safely, and that you are going to have to invest in taxi fares after all.

Finally, more simple to manage, it may be that you are expecting to use new technology to support your child academically into his new school. If he is going to be using a lap-top or palm-top computer, you will need to allow plenty of time now to make sure he is familiar with and confident with all the functions. If you are giving him a new mobile phone, make sure you do so in plenty of time for him to become fully sure of it. As far as possible, ensure everything new, whether clothing or technology, skills or increased independence, is faced now during the holidays so that it is no longer 'new' when school begins.

3.4 Taking on a project

One way to give the gap between schools something more of a structure is to take on a project. This can be anything, but one good idea is for it to be something associated with your child's specialist interest, or specialist subject (or both, if that is possible). If, for example, your child (like our Sam) has a passion for science, working together on a project logging the bio-diversity in your neighbourhood can be used to give a sense of optimism about the approaching opportunities for science at the new school (you could mention the powerful microscopes they have in school, the computer facilities for recording and analysing data, the opportunities for field work on trips). Conversely, if the project is on nothing 'school-y' at all, that is fine too. A project gives you a 'way in' to work with and interact with your child, and as such can set up the precedent for your helping your child with homework assignments when they start to come in (see section 4.5). More importantly, doing something like this together can give your time together a focus and a shared interest, and can be an opportunity to do something that has nothing whatsoever to do with changing school. Although you will be consciously 'managing' this holiday as a transition period, it is important that starting at the new school doesn't become an obsession. It is quite likely, given your child's diagnosis, that he will have an over-riding interest, and may quite possibly 'shelter' in this special interest, particularly when under stress. By joining in with him on a project to do with this you are both showing that you respect his interest and value it as a source of stress relief, and you are keeping communication open and allowing your child to talk to you (and at you!) about what interests him. If he switches to monologuing about his special interest when you want to review the map of the new school buildings, he may be trying to tell you something.

Your child's powerful preoccupation with his special interest may well increase during this period of transition. You may find that he spends longer organizing or cataloguing a collection, may feel even more driven to research his interest on the internet or to visit different airports to log arrivals of various planes. You may find that he 'monologues' at you about this interest more than previously, and that he seems almost to think of nothing else. If so, have the confidence that this is an effective coping technique, and respect his use of it. It may not be a passion that you share, but his intense absorption with his interest is providing him with order, with reassurance, with predictability and with enjoyment during this otherwise difficult period.

The other ongoing project that will be with both of you throughout this vacation is, of course, the transition plan. Make sure that you continue to update it, and allow plenty of opportunities for your child with AS to add questions if he wishes (and for you to come up with answers). Keep the approaching start of the new school 'out in the open', and don't allow it to become a dark thing that no one is mentioning. Keep calm and positive about it, and keep mentioning time on beyond that first day. If you are not careful, the first day will become the barrier to be overcome, with nothing beyond it. Mark the transition plan on into the months following, and make it clear that there will be plenty of opportunity on into that time to deal with things that are going wrong, to clarify confusions and to continue to give support.

3.5 Identifying and practising the different social 'rules' and expectations of the new school

Social rules and expectations are the hardest things to work on. They are incredibly subtle, and depend on things that we as parents (and even as adults) just fail to comprehend. Indeed, if we 'got' them, they would cease to be valid, for these are youth culture – and our youth has past!

For the child with AS, these social rules are exactly the things that he is most likely to get wrong. They are what makes 'fitting in' so difficult, and they are a problem because they are rules that are not written down, nor even set. They change, often according to quite precise and specific situations, and they are infinitely confusing.

To give an example: a (neuro-typical) child in one school I was observing had lost an eye in an accident. The other neuro-typical pupils at his school knew not to stare at him or to make too big an issue of this, but a pupil with AS was fascinated. He took great interest in the pupil's prosthetic eye, and asked innumerable questions. For this he was socially lambasted. The other students turned on him as insensitive and 'mean', and he was rejected by the whole peer group. Some work was done with him on not making personal comments and he learned to refrain, but the damage had been done.

Meanwhile, a student with high social standing, one of the group's natural leaders, responded by granting his 'protection' to the one-eyed student, and started calling him Cyclops. This naming of what had been unmentionable was done in a way that brought with it full acceptance of the pupil's one-eyedness, and inclusion of that pupil as someone of high social acceptance. The name was taken up by the boy's peers, and even on occasions by some teachers, as a recognition that this pupil's one-eyedness was now 'okay'. The one-eyed pupil thrived...but when the pupil with AS imitated his peers and used the nickname, he was again rejected by the group, who didn't give permission for him to use it. It could only be used affectionately by the pupil's friends, and they had decided that the pupil with AS had lost that right when he had earlier shown such tactlessness.

This example shows just how difficult it is to gain social acceptance in a complex social world. Unfortunately, no amount of direct teaching of the child with AS is ever going to explain these social rules, since they are unexplainable. What can be done, though, is some basic work on acceptance.

It is important, here, to enlist the help of a pupil who is already at the new school, and who has good social antennae. Find out from this pupil what at least the basic unwritten 'rules' are. There will be some. For example, they might include not wearing an outdoor coat, not doing up a jacket, carrying bags by one strap on the shoulder rather than by two on the back, not wearing the school scarf (even though the official rules say that you should). As an adult you might view these 'rules' with scepticism (How can it be right that 'everyone chews gum' when it clearly states in the school rules that gum is not allowed?), but it is nevertheless worth taking some of these social suggestions on board. Nothing is going to make your child with AS suddenly become 'trendy', but you may be able to prevent him from sticking out too obviously as someone with no social idea. If the fellow pupil says no scarf, don't make him wear one.

4

The First Days

4.1 Considering a flexi-start

One of the more controversial ideas on managing your child's start at school is to do so with a flexi-start. A flexi-start involves temporary use of flexi-schooling and involves allowing your child to 'dip his toe' into the chilly waters of school without the risk of getting drowned. Your child might begin by attending only registration sessions and perhaps assembly, might attend morning school but come home at lunch time, just attend in the afternoon or go in just for preferred lessons. It might be that any support he has been offered by the school could be concentrated on the times when he attends. The whole business of a flexi-start takes some organization, and not all schools will consider it. Those who disagree with the concept point out that this can lead to fragmentation, and to the child missing out on both lesson content and the vital early friendship-group-forming days at the beginning. These may be valid concerns, although lesson content can be made up perfectly well at home (indeed the child with Asperger syndrome (AS) may well learn better away from the challenges of coping with his new environment), and concerns around social dynamic-forming may be perceived through neuro-typical eyes and miss the effect of having AS.

In the early days of a group, where the dynamics of that group are being worked out, it can be an extremely tough environment. The members of the group, in this case children or adolescents – neither traditionally the most subtle or charitable of individuals – vie for position and evaluate each other against each other and against themselves. The strongest members of the group compete to be leaders, and in doing so will not allow themselves to be allied to those they perceive as weak. Later, when the dynamics are more firmly established, these strong characters are ideally placed to support more vulnerable individuals, but not until their own position is secure. In the cut-and-thrust of this early social manoeuvring, the child who is 'different' can be very vulnerable. Indeed, this different-ness will be far more likely to be noticed and far less likely to be tolerated. In these early days, the child with AS runs the risk of being spotted as 'odd' or 'weird', and this difference used in name-calling and taunting as individuals who are insecure themselves use these to distance themselves. These students may believe that they can only be 'in' the group if they are ready to exclude others as being 'outside' the group. In this intensely socially-orientated environment, the child with AS is unlikely to be included.

Curiously, though, this spotting of 'weirdness' or 'oddness' may not occur nearly as virulently if the individual admits to a difference. The child who says, 'I have autism' may be less likely to be victimized than the child who tries to hide his condition. It is as if the 'pretending to be normal' is the crime to the peer group, rather than the condition itself. It is also true, of course, that the child who accepts his own condition (and is confident with it) is less vulnerable than one who is ashamed of it and tries to hide it. There is nothing wrong with having autism or AS, and there is protection in law from anyone who says that there is.

The child who makes a 'flexi-start' to school has several advantages. One is that by doing so he is being open about his AS and therefore removing the need for others to point it out to him or others. This brings the AS 'out of the closet' and in doing so may reduce the likelihood that it will be used as a tool against him. Another is that school is only experienced in smaller, more manageable pieces. The child with AS need not be overwhelmed and is likely to be able to manage far better, be more confident, more sociable and happier for these shorter periods than if he had to deal with full days, day after day. Social acceptance will be greatly helped if, when the child is in school, he is managing 'well'. Conversely, if he becomes overwhelmed, this is when he is likely to get into fights, get into trouble with teachers, resort to self-stimulating or comforting behaviour (which is exactly the behaviour that is going to mark him out as 'odd' to his peers) or just quite simply shut down. None of these is going to help him, and some things are impossible to put right. If your child with AS becomes overwhelmed, loses skills and – for example – soils himself, then no amount of adult intervention or Teaching Assistant (TA) support is ever going to put that right. His chance of being accepted by his peers as having any sort of reasonable social standing during his years at that school is seriously jeopardized from that point onwards.

Whether you and/or your school consider flexi-schooling will depend a great deal on your personal circumstances and particularly on your child himself. If he is moving school with an already-established peer group, flexi-schooling may be inappropriate. If he is keen in no way to appear different, then it may not be something he would consider anyway. If you have work commitments that will not allow you the time for this period of flexibility, that too may make the idea impractical. If, however, you can manage the time and both you and your child are confident with his diagnosis, then it may be an idea worth talking about. It would give him a chance to build up his membership of this new school slowly, but in a way that is built on success. It is important to keep in mind a bigger picture. If he spends the first four or five weeks of his time at the school gradually building up his attendance, that may be a slightly unusual start. It is unlikely, though, to be remembered much beyond the first term, and by the time he has been at the school for five or six years, it will have been forgotten. If he goes straight into school using the 'fingers-crossed-and-hope-he'll-be-okay' technique of starting, he does run the risk of everything going horribly wrong, and of having to live with the consequences of that throughout the rest of his school life.

4.2 Using support

By the time your child starts at the new school you should be clear about how many hours of support, if any, he is going to be given. You will need to confirm with the school how his support is going to be managed. It may be that your child's dedicated support has, as it were, been submerged by general levels of support in the school. It is unlikely that he will have a nominated 1:1 assistant as he may have had at his previous school. Instead, his support may make up part of one TA's timetable at one part of the day, and of another's at another part of a different day. It is important that you keep track of this and make sure that your child is getting the support he needs.

Quite often, support is 'held as invisible' until it is seen to be needed. So, for example, your child may be provided a TA in a Science lesson, but not be aware that she is there particularly to help him. Instead she may provide general support across the whole lesson and only work directly with your child if he has need or gets into difficulty. This is fine, and means that the support offered to your child is more subtle and less overt, but you need to make sure that you are all clear what exactly 'gets into difficulty' or 'has need' mean to all parties. What you don't want is for support not to be forthcoming until your child hits crisis point. He doesn't need to be shouting, lashing out or escaping from the lesson before support should be put in place. Equally, he doesn't need to be 'failing' at the lesson. If your child is bright, and has the potential to be at the top of a class at a subject, then for him 'failure' is dropping down to become 'average'. Make sure that support is specific to your child's needs, able to be accessed by him without difficulty and supports him to be the best he can be.

It is likely to be a great deal more difficult to work with the people giving support, once your child moves up from a 1:1 system. When he had a dedicated TA, you had a chance to work with that person and to ensure that the messages you and she were giving your child were consistent. This is particularly important around issues of behaviour. Inconsistency may well be something that causes huge problems for your child with AS. For example, if you have agreed with him that he will take a book outside during break time, another adult tells him he must to go inside to read and a third takes the book away from him and tells him he should be getting some exercise, that is when you are going to get problems. It is hardly surprising that the child with AS becomes confused, withdrawn or resentful when the adults who work with him fail to communicate, and therefore to agree.

You will need to work hard with your 'named adult' to make sure that messages to your child are consistent. Although the school may have a strategy of using different TAs to support the same child over different lessons, there is nothing to stop you requesting that at least at first, he be given consistent support, or at least that the same person should support him consistently over the same lessons. If he knows that Miss F will help him in Art, that Mr A is available in History and Mrs P will support him over lunch times, at least he can begin to build up a consistent picture for each context. For further suggestions on helping your child to differentiate over different subjects and people, see section 4.4.

4.3 Checking his needs have been understood

After all of your hard work with your 'named adult' both before your child left his previous school and even, perhaps, over the holiday you may feel confident that your child's needs will be known and understood by his new school. This may, of course, be completely true…but it is as well to check. You have to be your child's ambassador if you are going to ensure that this transition to a new school really does go as smoothly as possible. Even if you are made to feel that you are intruding, you need to stay on your child's case. In this new environment, only you really know him. Until the new school has built up its expertise on what, precisely, your child's needs are, you are going to have to continue to be alert, to anticipate problems and prevent disasters. It is now, during these first few weeks, that much of your child's success or failure at this new school is likely to be decided, and you need to be vigilant to head off what might go wrong before it does.

The first days of a new school year are a busy time. Pupils are new and so are many staff, and all are new to each other. In this context, you may need to find a way to 'flag up' your child to his new teachers. As discussed in section 2.2, you may decide to use a quick and simple way to get your child introduced to his new teachers in the best possible way. The last thing you want is for your child's AS not to be taken into consideration at this early stage, for a teacher asserting his authority to use your child's confusion to make a point or an example. You need a way to protect your child in the mêlée of these busy, intense first few days.

One way to do this is to provide your child with a way of quickly and simply conveying information to his teachers. This information will need to be kept short and sharp and to be the absolute minimum that someone who doesn't know your child will need to know in order for your child to be 'okay'. For the moment, you are not trying to encapsulate every nuance of how to improve his education; instead you are providing a first introduction to what is essential. You might, for example, request that instructions be given directly, by name. You might ask that your child be given a nominated place in the classroom and so be told where to sit. You might ask that homework be written for him into his planner or that he be allowed to leave the room two minutes before the end of the class in order to make his way to the next lesson. Whatever it is you decide to target, it needs to be something that will be relevant over the different contexts he is likely to encounter, and which is a *positive* request for something that is *easy to deliver*. You are not, at this stage, drawing the teacher's attention to difficulties, but are providing one, easy, do-able and really helpful solution.

You can then have this request written up on a small card, able to be presented without fuss to each new teacher. It might read like this.

I am Michael Jones. I have Asperger syndrome.

Please allow me to leave class two minutes early in order to make my way to my next lesson.

Thank you.

Signed: Michael + SENCO/Form Teacher, etc.

This card does a number of things. It alerts the teacher to your son's condition, and identifies him as the child with AS who she was expecting in her class. It gives her a successful strategy, straight away, that will help your child and that will empower her as teacher. Immediately she has an easy, achievable strategy for differentiating for AS at her fingertips. By alerting her to your child's identity it means that she is far less likely to randomly pick your child to be the one to go first/read aloud/act out the scenario or whatever. She is also likely to make allowances from the start and be less likely to see unusual behaviour as defiant. Finally, it should awaken in her the need to go and read the files provided by you and your child's feeder school.

This first introduction is, of course, only the start. For example, you have considered your child's sensory needs already, (see section 2.6) and have discussed these with his 'named adult'. Now, though, you will need make sure that these needs are being met and understood on a day-to-day basis. Often, a new school will have a policy in place that is primarily reactive. In other words, the child with AS will be encouraged to join in the Drama lesson in the darkened studio or the Music lesson in the noisy classroom, and accommodation will only be put in place to support him if he shows 'need'. If he tolerates the environment, sits quietly and is not disruptive, it may be that he is considered to be 'okay'. I have even heard it said that children with AS 'need to learn to put up with discomfort' as if this approach is actually somehow beneficial to them.

There are a number of flaws in this philosophy. For a start, and at its most relevant for the school, such a strategy may simply just teach the child with AS that it is worth his while to 'kick off'. He may learn that behaving well and not causing any disruption means that he is not given access to differentiation to meet his needs. If he wants his sensory – or other – needs taken seriously, he is going to have to create a disturbance. Hitting out at or biting the person next to him should mean that the teacher in charge takes seriously that the lights are hurting his eyes.

Less obvious, the teacher may not understand to what extent sensory discomfort is reducing the performance of the child with AS. Bright lights, loud noises, darkness, strong smells…all may mean that the pupil is unable to take in other information, and that his learning is effectively blocked. It may well be that he shows no distress or disruptive behaviour at that time, but that does not mean that he is not affected. Perhaps he shuts down and finds it impossible to 'reawaken' next lesson, so that he appears dull and uncommunicative during a subject he would otherwise enjoy; perhaps he is so stimulated by the sensory overload that he finds it impossible to sit still during this next lesson, and is branded as 'naughty'; perhaps the smell makes him feel sick and unable to eat at lunch time, with a resulting drop in blood sugar and concentration in the afternoon. Only someone who is concerned with the pupil's overall welfare and who has the understanding to take sensory issues seriously is likely to be able to appreciate the real effect. You may well have to be this person until you can get staff at his new school to understand these issues.

Similarly, you may have asked that your child be allowed to use a computer, lap-top or word processor. This need will have to be followed up to make sure that the reasoning behind it is understood. It may be that your child 'appears' not to need it and to be coping with handwriting, and the fact that this requires an overwhelming effort that is blocking his ability to take in any other lesson content will only become apparent in a year's time when his results show that he is falling behind.

Usually, if your child's needs are not being met, it will be because of lack of AS understanding rather than any lack of willingness to help him. If you can make sure that his needs are really understood, that the effect of not meeting his needs is appreciated, the supports that you discussed earlier should be put in place. Continue to work closely with your named adult, and concentrate always on solutions and ways to help and support staff to meet your child's needs. With a bit of work it should be possible to ensure that the accommodations for him are put in place in the way you hoped they would be.

4.4 Providing practical and organizational support

Of course, much of what can be put in place to support your child with AS as he starts into his new school environment can be done by you without needing to alert the school at all. This 'background support' can be a huge source of help for your child, and can be a great way of keeping in touch with his needs as he experiences his new environment. It is essential that you keep lines of communication open with him, and working with him on the situation can be a good way to do this.

Once you have your copies of the school map and your child's timetable, you can go through each and colour code them. So, he may begin Monday morning with History (which you might shade in green), in room C12 (which you could then shade in green on the map). Your child may cope with the map being shaded with each colour as you identify the subject, but the result might be too 'busy' and difficult to read. Instead, you could copy the map many times. Shade Monday morning's History lesson in green, and mark on the map the route to the room from his class base where he has gone for registration. Then identify his next lesson – perhaps Technology – in red, and on the next map mark the Tech. room in red, together with the route from C12 to it. You will need a separate timetable for each day, attached to maps for each lesson. It may seem a lot of work, but clear, visual information at this time may be the most accessible for your child with AS, and knowing where he is going may alleviate much of the stress of his first days. Routes between classrooms, the rhythms of the day's timetable will become known eventually, and become familiar and able to be accessed subconsciously, without effort. Until that time, anything that helps to manage them has got to be useful.

The advantage of colour-coding subjects on the timetable is that you can extend the code to include other aspects. So, for example, you could cover History books in green paper, or at least provide a coloured strip on the spine if covering is not permitted. Homework assignments could be similarly coded, with the day they are to be handed in shaded appropriately in a homework diary. For a child who has difficulty memorizing the timetable, the day's lessons, once colour coded, can be presented visually on a key fob. Choose the colours for the lessons with your child. Cut out and laminate strips in each colour, and hole punch. Before school each morning, order the laminated strips into the order of the school day and slip onto the key fob. Simple, visual prompts such as this are easy to manage and can be hugely reassuring for a pupil with AS. All that is needed is some imagination and a clear understanding of what your child's needs are at this time.

Incidentally, do not be surprised if your child's needs at this time, during the transition into a new school, are considerably greater than you are used to. It is hard for we who are not starting a new school to fully appreciate the demands, the confusions, the concentration, the problem-solving or the downright effort that are involved. If we do not have AS, how much harder is it for us to understand it from an AS perspective? Your child may not have needed constant reassurance about what exactly would happen and when at his old school. He probably won't need such reassurances, either, when he has fully settled at this one, but for now he may need such reassurance a great deal. Simple visual prompts, however you choose to manage them, can help enormously, and are supports that we as parents are able to put into place for our children without having to rely on others. Sometimes it helps us to help, and that shouldn't be discounted either.

One of the challenges facing your child in his new school is that he is likely to encounter a far greater range of teachers than he is used to. Perhaps at his old school he had one class teacher, with perhaps another teacher for Maths or PE. Now he may well have a change of teacher for every lesson, perhaps even every half an hour. In the course of the day he may have to deal with many different adults, and each will have different rules, different expectations and different ways of working. This is a challenge for the pupil with AS.

You can help by working with your child, with other pupils if you know them, with the Special Educational Needs Coordinator (SENCO) and with the teachers themselves to record these different rules and expectations. As discussed in section 2.4, you could make up a Teacher

Book with different teachers' photographs, their names, subjects and particular quirks and rules. You could make a card that slips into the front of each subject's book, and on it give the subject (colour coded) and the teacher's name and, if possible, photograph. You would then need a series of sections to be completed. These would vary depending on different schools, but might include the following:

- before the lesson (e.g. line up outside or go into the room?)

- seating (e.g. nominated seats or sit where you like?)

- preferred mode of address (e.g. Sir? Mr Smith?)

- clothing (e.g. jackets on or off? Lab coats, art overalls, cooking aprons?)

- equipment needed for lesson (e.g. books, pens or pencils, calculator?)

- homework rules (e.g. give in at start of lesson? Wait until it is collected?)

- end of lesson (e.g. go when bell sounds? Wait until dismissed? Stand behind chairs at bell?).

It is helpful if the teacher or support staff can help to complete this list, not least because it helps them to realize Asperger needs and that these are the pupil's expectations from then on. The pupil should not get into trouble for failing to hand in work at the beginning of the lesson if the subject 'rule' is to wait until asked for it to be collected. This is also an ideal vehicle to request a more structured, formalized approach for the child with AS. Having a nominated place to sit in each classroom, for example, can be a great help, and can prevent the anxiety of not knowing where to sit or sitting in the 'wrong place' (perhaps next to someone who doesn't want him to, or inadvertently in the section of the classroom usually occupied by a certain group or gang). Teachers can struggle to know how best to help pupils with AS who come into their care, and fairly simple approaches like these can be a great help for everyone.

4.5 Monitoring and supporting homework

One of the traditional ways for parents to get involved and to help their child at school is with the business of homework, and this is true also for the parents of the child with AS…only more so. Homework can cause considerable stress for the student with AS. No one likes doing homework, but for your child it is likely to be more than this. It may be that, having managed to get through these first days and arrive safely home, he cannot face the contamination of his home environment by doing work from school. This need to keep one environment (home) safe, controlled and unsullied is understandable. He may desperately need to recharge after considerable confusions and demands during his school day. Bringing school work into his sanctuary may be more than he can bear.

It may also be the case that he has no real concept of what homework is demanded. If he has found the lesson confusing already, if he has been mechanically following instructions with no real understanding of the underlying point of what he is doing, he may have little idea of what is required for homework. Most students are able to deduce the purpose behind what is set. Is it to finish off this piece of work because a new one will be started next lesson? Is it to do some preparation for a topic to be addressed next lesson? Is it, frankly, because homework is expected and is more or less a 'time-filler'? With their understanding of the purpose behind the homework will come some confidence in the neuro-typical mind about how much work is needed, how long it should take and what is expected by it. Neuro-typical students are likely to be pretty quick to develop an unwritten but very potent personal understanding of the minimum homework that they can do and get away with it!

The student with AS may have none of these things. For him, homework as set may well be literally un-'doable'. Terms like 'Finish this off' hold no clues about how much work is needed. 'See what you can find out' is so open-ended that the student with AS may perceive that he is being asked to study the subject to PhD level. Even fairly simple instructions such as 'Answer questions 1 to 5' may not give all the information the student with AS requires. How is he supposed to answer them? Should he write the answers down, and if so, where? In how much detail does the teacher require him to answer them? If he doesn't know an answer, is he permitted to look the answer up or would that be 'cheating'?

The first place to go to for support with homework is likely to be the school. Many schools offer homework clubs, either during lunch and break time or after school. Accessing such a club during school time may have the added advantage of giving your child something to do and somewhere safe to go during these unstructured times. The homework club will almost definitely be staffed, and this should mean that there is an adult who is well placed to clarify homework demands. Especially if she knows your child, she may be able to structure a vague instruction into three specific steps, and set time or space parameters for each step. This is likely to be even more successful if he is able to access support in the safe haven during these times, and so get help from staff with a good AS understanding.

If your child is still arriving home with work to do, you will need to decide your attitude to homework. Some parents swear by homework as a vital ingredient to a successful education. Others see it as a complete waste of time. You are going to decide where you stand on the issue.

If you decide that your child has plenty of other demands to contend with, and that this is one battle you can all do without, you have two options. One is to approach the school and request that homework not be set for your child, at least for this initial transition period. You may be able to explain to the school why his AS means that homework, at least for the moment, is more than he can manage. However, you may find that the completion of homework, and parental support for its completion, are enshrined within the school prospectus and there is no way you are going to be able to avoid it. Often work is 'piled on' to pupils at the beginning of their time at a school, simply in order to establish that there is now an expectation that they do it. If this is the case at your new school, it is likely that there will be no escape from it. In this case, it might be best to simply do the homework yourself!

Actually, this is not quite the facetious suggestion that it sounds, especially if you do it with your child in attendance. Working on your child's homework can be a good way of keeping 'in touch' with him and his school life, and it is tangible proof for him that you understand how hard this transition is for him and that you will do everything in your power to help. Going through the work as it is set gives you a chance to spot concepts that he may have misinterpreted or just plain misunderstood. Even if you are giving this support, though, it may be best to find a place to do the work that is separate from the rest of 'home'. You might use your public library or allow your child to come into your place of work and stay back together for half an hour of an evening to get the work done. If you have to do the work at home, try to find a place that is kept specifically for the purpose, whether that be a study or just a table in a corner, and have a set time and time limit for the work. It may be far more manageable for your child with AS if he knows that school will only intrude on home during one hour, between five and six, and that after that he will regain his home as the sanctuary he needs. In time, as he settles at the school, you should be able gradually to hand the responsibility for homework back to him... although you may always find it a thorny issue.

4.6 Helping with management of workload

The other side of homework, of course, is to make it work for you and most of all for your child. An early homework, as the child starts at the school, may well be the setting of some sort of longer project. What is being tested, here, is likely to be as much the student's ability to organize his time as the content of what he produces – and it may well be that your child's inability to organize himself or his time is one of the symptoms of his condition. This longer project, then, may be a real challenge, but may equally provide a golden opportunity to actually work on a skill that is very relevant to your child. If you view it as a helpful chance to confront one of your child's weaknesses and to find ways both to accommodate and to work around his difficulties, it can seem a great deal more welcome and relevant.

It may be that there is little point in setting your child the task as it is presented. 'Complete a project, involving at least 12 hours of study, on an environmental issue of your choice' may, as it stands, be simply a disaster waiting to happen. Helping to fend off that disaster is not cheating, nor is it irresponsible. Using the project to work with your child on an accessible and repeatable technique to manage a challenge such as this is proper education. Don't let the opportunity slip away.

You will need to quantify how much work is needed (in this case it is given, 12 hours, but it may not always be), how many pages of project that will be translated into, when the work is due in, how long away that is and therefore how much work needs to be done each week. Decide when each week the work will be done, for example half an hour on Mondays and half an hour on Wednesdays. Work out how many sessions that will be. Choose the topic together (your child may need considerable help in this as very open-ended choices such as this may have just too many possibilities to be managed), and break the work needed into the number of sessions available. Articulate very clearly what is needed to complete each session. When the project is under way, monitor it carefully and do your best to keep it to the schedule. You may need to provide practical support, such as collecting the work from each session and keeping it safe and in order. At the end of the project, again provide practical support in sorting the work out, compiling it and presenting it effectively. Value the result, and encourage your child to see the result as valuable too.

What you are doing in this case is a great deal more than helping to produce a 'long homework' on an environmental issue. You are providing a blue-print of how to manage a longer project. If you can support your child with AS to successfully complete a longer, multi-faceted task such as this, you are giving him a life skill that will stand him in excellent stead into the future. Take as many opportunities as you can to generalize the skills your child has just learned across different contexts. Even if another long project is not forthcoming at school, you may perhaps be able to manufacture one. Perhaps you could persuade one of his subject teachers to accept a 'long homework' such as this in place of what is set on a daily basis. Even if you cannot find a school-based way of repeating the experience, you could show your child how you use a similar technique to plan for a holiday, or go about choosing the components for a new bathroom. Draw his attention back to the transition plan. Didn't that use very much the same way of working?

Your help in this project allows you to adapt what has been set to make it a far more useful educational experience for your child. Much of what your child experiences in school will be irrelevant to him, and will cause difficulty and confusion. Some of this can be used to help him to better understand the neuro-typical world and to adapt to it. Others, like this, can be turned around to present a more Asperger-suitable learning opportunity. Part of your job, as you help your child to make sense of this new environment, is to filter his various experiences to make sure that what emerges is as positive a learning experience as possible for your child.

4.7 Facilitating communication

One of your biggest challenges, once your child with AS has actually started at the school, is to find out how he is doing. You may have to rely on what he tells you, and that may not be very informative. Even neuro-typical children seldom give detailed feedback on the school day ('What did you do at school today?' 'Oh – nothing.'). If you think about it, the question, especially for the Asperger mind is impossible to answer. What did I do at school? What, do you mean every second?

To complicate matters, your child with AS may not be aware of how well he is doing or when he is starting to run into problems. He may feel that he has followed instructions in lessons, has done the work demanded, is making friends...and this may not be at all the viewpoint of the other members of the school. His various teachers may be slowly pulling their hair out as he produces eccentric, irrelevant or indeed no work, and classmates may be taunting, or setting him up, and not being friendly at all. This is a darkest view of course, but it is a possible scenario and the point is, you may not know.

If you are to remain proactive and involved in your child's transition, you are going to have to remain fully aware of what happens during his days at school. You are going to have to stay accessible to help to fend off problems, and stay aware of what is going on if you are going to help your child to negotiate around the pitfalls. It is also likely to be a great help if you can use your communication skills to help compensate for your child's weakness in this area. He may not understand that he is being asked to finish the project for homework, just because the term used was 'in your own time', but you will, and can help to get that work done before your child ends up in trouble.

If it can be said that you may not be aware of problems that are brewing, and nor is your child, it may also be true that staff, unfamiliar with your child, may themselves not spot potential difficulties as they arise. Very often the child with AS gets 'lost' in school because he appears to be managing adequately. If he is not lashing out or being disruptive, if he doesn't complain and is producing some work, albeit to a fairly low standard, he may find that he drifts through years of schooling without anyone really engaging with his difficulties. What is sad is that this sort of experience is often held up by a school as being a 'success' for a child with AS. If he achieves invisibility then presumably he's doing okay and no one sees any problem. It may be years into adulthood that his frustrations, loneliness, low self-esteem and lack of skills and qualifications are identified as problems, and traced back to an inadequate education experience.

If you are going to prevent this from happening, you are going to have to keep communication channels open. Fortunately, communication is developing all the time and we have so many more ways of 'keeping in touch' these days than did the previous generation. With e-mail, texting, mobile phones, SMS messaging, voice alerts and the whole host of other communication facilities, it should be easier to keep in touch than it used to.

For a start, even though your child disappears into school, you can stay in touch. He can text you if he is lost or unsure, and you are able to respond immediately, rather than hoping that he can remember the problem and articulate it to you at the end of the day. At least for this transition period you could, perhaps, make conscious time available through each day when you are available to him to offer this support. Even more useful than contacting you, of course, is if your child with AS could text his named adult in school. A good special needs support team may be able to keep communication open all the time, and provide a constant service where they can be contacted and provide instant reassurance and information. If they don't provide this, it may be worth requesting. Failing that, you may need to act as an exchange. Allow your child to text or phone you, make a clear list of the matters that are puzzling or alarming him and take them up with the school yourself. Again, you have clearer communication skills than your child and are likely to be better placed to articulate concerns.

Good communication works both ways. If your child's teachers can contact him by e-mail, this may be an ideal tool to use to clarify homework requirements, or to give prior warning of changes in routines. If a member of staff knows that she will be away and that a substitute teacher will be taking the class tomorrow, sending the child with AS this information, together with a reassurance that the new teacher is aware of your child's specific concerns or needs, can be a huge help. Schools that have a good, constantly updated school website can provide this sort of service to all pupils. Often, what supports a child with AS will actually be very helpful for a number of children, which is of course one of the many advantages of children with AS being present in a school.

Before the transition to the new school, you were working hard to open channels of communication between your child's old and new schools. Try to keep those open now that the child has moved. The previous school still has a wealth of expertise on your child that has yet to be built up in this new context. Although staff at the old school will have moved on and have other children to be caring for now, you need to try to not lose that expertise. Perhaps you could request that a TA who worked closely with your child before could come across and see how he is doing in his new placement. Perhaps a TA assigned to work with him now could go across to his old school and ask questions about the best ways of supporting him. Schools tend to be closed societies with 'their own way of doing things'. You need to combat this attitude if at all possible if your child is not to find himself right back at the beginning, with the same old mistakes being made again and again.

Of course, ultimately your child's continuity of care is going to rest with you. You will need to discuss with the school when (and how) they are going to call on you for help. Many good schools are ready to call on the parents as a matter of routine if a child is struggling. Others, sadly, seem to feel that they have to resolve all matters internally and that it would somehow be admitting failure to turn to the parents of a child for help with that child. Try to get the school to agree a policy that they will call you quickly in if your child is in difficulties. Don't let this become a confrontational matter, where calling the parents in is seen as being the last resort for a disruptive, uncontrollable child. Hard though it may be for the school to understand, this is a partnership and if all of you have your child's welfare firmly at heart, there is a great deal you can do to support each other and help to achieve that best result.

The person who you need to be most 'constant' with is your child. In a world where all else has changed, your continued maintenance of routines, of structures and supports will be hugely important. Even if it is only a matter of having a secure routine around bed time, or of having a predicable, timetabled set of meals (always macaroni cheese on Thursdays, always shepherd's pie on Mondays), you can provide security and stability in an otherwise very tempestuous world.

4.8 Ensuring that the 'simple' supports are in place (and remain so)

You are likely to have spent considerable time with your child's named adult, prior to the change of schools, discussing his needs. What may have happened is that these discussions became quite abstract, a discussion of provision that could be put in place in theory, and you will need now to make sure that all that philosophy has actually been translated into practical support.

For example, you probably discussed the existence of a safe haven that your child could access during unstructured times such as break and lunch and also when he felt he needed to in a crisis. You may find that this has been made available to your child at agreed points in the day, but that ways to access the haven in a crisis have not been discussed (or, perhaps, encouraged).

As well as firmly established and articulated rules about when it is acceptable to make routine use of the safe haven, it might be as well to request that your child be allowed a card that grants him access, even during lesson time. If he is becoming stressed or overwhelmed, his communication skills may be the first thing to fail him. It is asking a lot to expect him to request to leave a class and to articulate why he needs to. More effective is a card that can be used like a 'get-out-of-jail-free' card, often called an Exit Card. It might be printed with a direction from the SENCO or your child's form tutor requesting that, on presentation of the card, your child always be allowed to leave class and make his way to the safe haven. If such a card is permitted, and its use honoured at all times, most of the crisis points and flare-ups that seem characteristic of the child with AS who is finding school difficult may be avoided.

Clearly the acceptance of the card will require some background work by the school. Agreement will have to be reached on where your child should go, how long he stay there, who he should contact and so on. It also requires a commitment from your child that he will not abuse the trust implied by the card. If he has presented the card he must, for example, always make his way directly to the agreed place. Nor must he use the card as an exit strategy for activities that he finds merely uninteresting rather than distressing. Much of the success of an Exit Card relies on quality follow-up to its use. Time must always be made available to discuss what situation prompted the need to use the card, and what can be done to alleviate that situation. It is also important that work missed is always made up and that difficulties and confusions are resolved. For many teachers the Exit Card will appear to be an unnecessary indulgence. They may be reluctant to honour it, and considerable education may be needed to make them understand the reason for its use. The focus should not be on whether the child should be allowed to leave the lesson; the focus should be on finding an acceptable way to communicate the need to leave the lesson. The alternative to using the card may well be that the child uses other techniques. If he swears, hits out, spits, breaks equipment, howls, cries or wets himself, he will usually find himself able to exit a class. He could also exit, of course, by merely running out of the door. The Exit Card, and the respect between each of the parties that it implies, is a much better solution.

Many of the supports that you discussed with your named adult during the period prior to moving schools may have been rather simpler than this. Perhaps you, or your child's previous school, articulated that he would be helped by being allowed to leave class early in order to make his way to the next lesson. Perhaps you agreed that he would be given a nominated place to sit in each class, or that teachers be aware of the need to write his homework assignments down for him in his planner. Perhaps you requested something as simple as 'name before instruction', or a specific way that your child could ask for clarification if he were unsure.

What you will need to do is to ensure that these strategies are, indeed, being put in place, and that they are continued. Quite often, differentiation may be made for a student with AS for the first few days, but it is soon assumed that he no longer needs it unless he shows overt signs of distress. You may have to work with the school to understand that the period of transition, for a child with AS, is likely to be longer than for his neuro-typical peers, and so too is the period for which he will need extra support. Indeed, they should be aware that some of these supports may well be needed indefinitely. You are going to have to be proactive in ensuring that everyone understands that the need behind the differentiations that you request remains, however 'well' the child may be doing, and will continue to be present, and that he may continue to need this sort of differentiation throughout his school life – and indeed throughout his life to come.

For example, a student with AS may be permitted to leave class early to make his way to his next lesson for the first few days, while he is becoming familiar with his new environment, but then no longer be permitted to do so when it is assumed that he knows his way around. However, although the route may have become familiar to the pupil with AS, the jostle and claustrophobia of many bodies in a confined space may mean that changing lessons with everyone else remains problematic. His need to go early, while corridors and stairways are quiet, is not primarily to do with finding his way, but to do with managing as he makes that way. This may very well continue to be the case.

With this in mind, it may be a good idea to keep careful note of all the various supports that are being put in place as your child starts into his new school. If to begin with he is 'doing well', but things start to fall apart after the first week or so, one possibility is that his support is being withdrawn, even subconsciously. Go back to the school and ask that what was in place is put back. If your child's behaviour, attainment or general happiness again improve, you have a strong case for arguing that the support is still needed.

4.9 Accessing transition support from 'Asperger community' of school

As already mentioned in section 2.13, one of the greatest sources of Asperger understanding during this time may well be other students in the school with an autistic spectrum disorder (ASD). Once your child is in school, both you and he are likely to find it easier to access this support from other students. It may have been hard to identify these students before your child started at the school, as the school might have felt that it was breaking confidentiality to put you or your child in touch with them. Now that he is a member of the school community, this support should be far more forthcoming, and with it a source of support for you from other parents in a similar position. As a community you will have a stronger voice than merely as individuals.

Your child may find that he accessing this support community almost without realizing it. If the school operate a policy of providing a safe haven during unstructured time, it is quite possible that your child will become familiar with other students already accessing this haven. Perhaps, as time goes on, he may begin to realize that the same group of people meet in the haven each lunch time, and – like him – several of them are 'into' computer games or card collecting, or are bright and 'wordy' or indeed clumsy and poor at team sports. This is a natural way for a community to form, and can be highly successful. Without anyone forcing it, a group of students begin to recognize themselves as sharing a common identity.

If this is not happening naturally, it may be worth your while finding out why. It is unlikely in most school communities that your child will be the only one with AS or a similar diagnosis on the autistic spectrum, and if the other students with this diagnosis are hard to find, it may be that the school ethos encourages an atmosphere of keeping such a diagnosis a secret. This is unlikely to encourage a positive attitude towards having AS, and you might like to question it. Of course, it is up to each individual with AS or any ASD to decide how widely he shares that diagnosis, but for many students it may not be in the least something to be 'ashamed of' unless they have been made to feel that it is. A more open, respectful, even celebratory attitude from the school community as a whole might well be something that could be worked on.

If the AS community has been allowed to develop, within it there are many opportunities for ways to help your child with AS in this transition. For example, it may be possible for an older pupil with AS to mentor your child, perhaps explaining the pitfalls and giving encouragement in ways to manage AS within this society of school. To make this sort of mentoring and positivity really work, the school need to take on that this community has an identity of its own in much the same way as a religious or ethnic community might do. Each has a duty towards respect for the larger community as a whole, and of its rules and traditions, but each further has a right to respect for its own needs and customs.

If the AS community is going to be nurtured and encouraged to support its members itself, it is unlikely to do so without the active encouragement of the school. If the school is really ready to embrace this philosophy, though, there is a wealth of advantages. Many of the 'difficult' areas for the student with AS – social integration, dating, personal hygiene, bullying, social empathy, 'tact' and so on – can be explored within an AS context. It should be possible to allow students within the AS community to come together to explore many of these topics together. This is an opportunity to bring in outside autism/Asperger expertise, and to help the students to explore just what their diagnosis means for them now and on into the future. This dynamic, active approach to 'managing' AS within the school community is likely to lead to success for everyone.

4.10 Evaluating the first days

One of your tasks as the first days for your child in his new school slip by is to keep some sort of evaluation of how it is all going. It is important that you do this from everyone's perspective. Do the school think it is going well? Do you? Most importantly, does your child with AS?

What is needed is some sort of active way of gathering feedback. Waiting for your child to articulate that there is a problem is not a good idea. He may not be able to express concerns, or not even be aware that they are things about which he should make an expression. Perhaps he takes a level of discomfort, of loneliness or anxiety as a 'norm', and never thinks to challenge it. Perhaps his relief at getting home each day is so great that he is unwilling to think back over his school day and talk about what has been happening. He may live very much in the present, and lack the social skills necessary to articulate concerns or disappointments. He may, quite simply, not see the point in stating what has happened. A person with AS may lack the empathy to understand that your experience differs from his. He may believe that because he knows what happened today at school, you will know too.

What is needed, then, is a simple and effective way of gaining this feedback, without too much of an issue being made about it. It may be best to use a visual method, and to avoid anything that is too wordy or too abstract. 'How was school?' is probably a daft question to someone with AS. You are going to have to be far more specific than that.

One way to assess how your child feels about facing each new day is to add a simple, visual way of recording this into your daily planning. You may, for example, have created a system where the day's events are clearly displayed, for example on a whiteboard in your kitchen. You might have a system that says 'Monday', then states homework to be handed in that day, lists the lessons (colour coded) with equipment needed, and indicates any other variables such as how your child is travelling to/from school that day, any events planned for the evening and so on. Such a system would certainly be beneficial in helping your child to be organized and prepared for his day. To this, you could add a series of emoticons – perhaps even just a smiley face, a neutral face and a sad face. Ask your child to add the emoticon at the top of the board. This should give you some idea of how he is feeling about that day.

More sophisticated would be to have a whole range of descriptive words, perhaps as fridge magnets, and to ask that he puts one on his planner to indicate how he feels about the coming day. In amongst a range of fairly neutral words ('bored', 'interested', 'nervous', 'excited', 'okay', 'optimistic') you could hide a couple of red-letter words such as 'frightened' or 'despairing'. Although it is to be hoped that he wouldn't choose these words too frequently in earnest, if he does at least that gives you some warning.

Another approach is to devise a way to record how things are going, as your child goes along. This might seem too general a concept for your child, so you could make it more specific by encouraging him to use a system for recording both good and bad experiences. The little adhesive coloured dots that you can buy in most stationers can be a great way to do this. Agree a code with your child, perhaps green to indicate a calm lesson, yellow a really good one and black a terrible one. You could add in red to indicate if he felt angry. Encourage him to add a dot (or dots) after lessons on his daily planner, if he feels that there is a need. This will give you a useful resource for going back over his day with him and sorting out any problems that have occurred.

You could request a similar system with your child's teachers. You don't want to give them extra work, nor to make it feel as though your child is 'on report' (used by many schools as an indication of unacceptable behaviour or attitude). However, an easy, quick and visual way of recording that there has been a concern can be very helpful. Problems and difficulties could then be picked up easily by the school in form time, or through contact with your child's named adult. All these are ways of facilitating communication and finding ways for all the parties involved to monitor and express their experiences of school. Without this sort of conscious recording method in place, the 'small' problems or incidents in your child's day are likely to be lost...and so run the risk of becoming bigger. If either your child, or his teachers, have a quick and time-efficient way to record an issue, that means that a misunderstanding, a failure to interpret an instruction correctly, an apparent rudeness or act of defiance can be picked up quickly, before problems develop. Although it may seem to be adding yet another thing to your child's teachers that you are asking them to do, in fact it is giving them an opportunity to seek clarification that may not otherwise be easy to get. Each of them is likely to be finding their feet as they learn how best to interact with your child, and how best to accommodate his AS, and a simple system such as this, that allows even small queries to be followed up, may in fact be very welcome.

The other party, of course, who needs to record how well the transition is going is you as parent. A simple record of some kind that indicates when your child appears calm, when withdrawn, when volatile and easily upset and so on will be a useful record to look back on. If you are keeping a record of changes in your child's moods or behaviours, you are in a good position to record patterns. Perhaps you realize that he is always more restless and tetchy on a Tuesday evening, or that it is harder to get him out of the door on time and well prepared on a Thursday morning. Each gives you something to work on to find out what the issues are. Equally (and more positively), you may realize that, although he is still apprehensive on a Monday morning, in fact he is managing well once the week is up and running. You need to know when *not* to worry as well as when to do so.

5

Into the Future

One of the more useful things you can do at this time is to provide an evaluation of the whole transition process, both for your child's current and for his previous school. Such feedback would ideally, have been available for you to see when you were first looking at schools, and indeed when you first approached your child's previous school to discuss the business of transition. If you can give good, clear, mostly positive feedback but with some practical suggestions on ways to make the process even better, you will be doing the next pupil with Aspreger Syndrome (AS) (and his parents) a favour, and will be helping both schools to take their transition support for such students seriously.

You could, for example, go through the check-list in the Appendix of this book. Which of these were you offered? Which were most useful? Would you like to have been offered any that were not, and did you find any that were offered less than useful? Perhaps you were offered different transition support. If so, did it work? Your feelings, as a parent of a child with AS, are hugely important and your current level of expertise, having just gone through the process, should not be lost. Of course, it may be that either or both schools already have an assessment of their transition support in place. If so, that in itself is to be commended. If not, your willingness to provide feedback, your request that they should seek your evaluation, may be enough to prompt the school or schools to put these things into place.

Of course, the ideal evaluation would not contain feedback just from you as parents, but from the staff at both schools, from autism or other health professionals working with your child and indeed and most importantly from your child himself. If the dangers of getting this transition wrong – with the associated danger of school failure and therefore of unhappiness, depression, low self-image, academic failure and ultimate lack of qualifications and independent skills – are to be taken seriously, the way the transition is managed should itself be given a high profile. It matters. By feeding back to the schools on what they did that worked, and on what they might have done which could have worked better, you are helping to give this process some of the importance it deserves.

Your child has a great deal to add to this. Much has been said in this book about accessing the existing AS community in the school. Even if you have not found this to exist, you and your child are currently ideally placed to put supports into place to help the next pupil with AS making transition. Could your child be the one to go to the feeder school and assess the changes facing the pupil as he moves up (see section 2.9)? Could your child help write a 'Guide to moving to School X for the pupil with AS', or at least come up with the 'Three Top Tips' mentioned in section 2.13?

One of your tasks, together with your child and with the school, is to set a limit as to when 'transition' will end. Does transition between school cover the last term at the previous school and the first at the new? Is it an intense period of days, or a longer one of weeks – or is it a process that spans months? If you have been thinking in terms of a '2-year plan', of a long-term project that has taken considerable amounts of your time and energy, it may be hard to realize that you have, in fact, reached the end of this process.

As your child has been going through this process, he may also have felt very much that he has been vulnerable, has been someone who 'doesn't know'. Expressing that the transition is over and requesting that he helps to create some transition evaluation feedback could be a great way for him to round off the whole transition process. Asking him to come up with ideas and strategies to improve the process and to help others who will be making the journey in later years may help to say to him that he has 'done it', that he has achieved transition and is through to the other side. Of course, this is not the end to all problems, but it is an end to those transition-specific problems. This closure itself may be hugely beneficial to all.

It would, of course, be naïve to suggest that if your child with AS is able to make a successful transition to his new school, all problems and challenges for him will be over. Having crossed over the bridge, he will still find himself at the school and will still be faced with all that that entails. However, transition behind him, he will now be a member of that new community and that community, with him and with you his parents, will face the challenges of how to best manage his membership together.

It will, indeed, be very hard if, when the period you had mentally assigned yourself for this transition has passed, your child is still not settled and not happy. You may begin to despair. What are you to do if he adds a black dot after each day or puts a sad emoticon on every morning? What if the school are contacting you to complain about his behaviour? What if each day you have to prise his fingers off the door frame even to get him out of the door? How long a 'settling in' period are you going to allow?

It is important, always, to keep in mind how hard all of this is for your child, and to be patient. For all the reasons already discussed in Csection 1.1 this change of schools is likely to have been a huge challenge for him. Were it not, this book would not have been written and, perhaps more importantly, you would not have felt the need to read it. We as parents of a child with AS know how difficult all of this is likely to be. We are taking it seriously. The premise behind this book has been that, as long as sufficient and appropriate support and understanding is available, a child with AS can be helped to make a successful transition between schools. You must have believed in the school to have worked so hard to get your child to settle at it. What you will need to do is to hold onto that belief as you continue to offer your child support.

If you have followed much of what is suggested in this book you will have been providing considerable support for your child. You will have prepared him, both before he left his old school and through the holidays, you will have helped him to develop the skills necessary to make the transition and you will have ensured that appropriate support has been put in place in school and maintained there. If your child is really not coping, you may need to go back over these strategies and revisit them.

It may well help to continue to use your transition plan. Show your child the journey he has travelled along and the various ways you have answered questions and addressed concerns together. Show him how he was articulating questions by putting them up on the board and how you were finding answers together. Encourage him to continue to use this strategy. Reassure him that, whatever it is that he is finding difficult, it can be addressed and probably resolved. Remind him of your promise about bullying. If he is actually frightened of going into school, reassure him that you will not send him into danger and that you will take concerns seriously. You are going to have to remain the constant in this confusing and shifting world. He has to be a able to believe that he can trust you and that you can 'sort it out'. Keep your doubts about this to yourself. He needs your confidence and your strength.

If you did not consider a flexi-start originally, it may be that this is a strategy you may have to try now. If 'total immersion' into school is not working, it may be better to pull your child out a bit and let him cope with what he finds difficult one thing at a time. It is better to put things right, even one by one, than to let problems accumulate and threaten to overpower him.

If flexi-schooling, even temporarily, is not an option for you (or, indeed, if the school will not allow it which might be the case), you are going to have to find another way to take the pressure off your child while he adjusts. One way might be to request that he drops certain subjects, at least for now, and has that time in the safe haven each day in order to recharge. He might be allowed books or his collection around his current special interest, and may find that spending 'off' time like this is enough to enable him to return afterwards to the fray. If you have managed to identify certain subjects, or even certain teachers, as problem areas for your child, these might be the ideal ones to drop for now. This is not to pander to his weaknesses. If he can get the rest of his school life 'together', he will be in a much stronger position to work on what he finds difficult. Expecting to do everything all at once is clearly not, in this case, working for him.

Another thing to check is that his unstructured time is not causing difficulty. For many students with AS, the time when they are not in lessons, and therefore where fewer official rules apply, may be far more difficult for them. This is the time when a student with AS may, literally, not know what to do, and it is the time when he is most vulnerable. Bullying and taunting are also more likely to take place during this less-supervised time. You have requested that your child have access to a safe haven during these times. Is that happening? One school I visited said that they did not allow vulnerable students to access their safe haven during break times because 'they (the staff) needed their break too'. This sort of attitude is precisely why you need to stay vigilant and to make sure that your child's needs are indeed being addressed.

If you can find out from your child what the problem is, you have a chance of working with him and with the school to come up with a solution. Remember, this does not have to be a solution that will stay in place forever. Dropping a subject temporarily is very different from dropping it forever. What everyone needs to keep in mind is that you are dealing here with transition and that transition is going to take some time. Be patient, and continue to believe that, in the end and with proper accommodation, your child can be happy at this school.

If your child's unhappiness is more amorphous, it may be more difficult to address. It may simply be that your child does not 'feel right' yet at the school. It takes a long while to redraw a mental map with new experiences firmly embedding in it. While the school sounds strange and smells strange, while it looks unfamiliar, but the people in it are not known and familiar, it may simply be that it is a hostile environment for your child with AS. Continue your work on walking round the school after the other students have gone. Encourage your child to take more photographs and to become really familiar with the map of the school. Fill in your child's Teacher Book (see section 2.4 and section 4.4) together and work together to decode various teachers' strange behaviours. If such a thing exists, get hold of a class or year-group photograph. How many students can your child identify? Which ones has he ever sat next to? Which ones are good at your child's favourite subject in school?

You will need to be aware that your child is likely to be extremely tired during these early days at school. Some, at least, of his despondency may be rooted in exhaustion. Limit any outside activities, make sure that he gets to bed early and also that he is getting plenty of sleep (which is not the same thing). Keep foods familiar and predictable to avoid hunger or an upset digestion. Tempting though it is, try not to try to take his mind off his current predicament with treats and outings. The familiar and the constant are likely to be the most reassuring during this time.

If your child is unhappy, set a time – visually, on his transition plan – by which time you believe he will have settled or else you will take further action. Part of the overwhelming problem with school for all children is its 'forever-ness'. Reassure your child by marking this date that this unhappiness will not, in fact, go on forever. You are taking it seriously. By marking a date on the calendar, and by continuing to stay fully involved, you may be able to give your child the space he needs to find his place at the school.

Of course, by doing so you are going to have to decide what you will do if he continues to be actively unhappy at that time. By then you may have had to decide what problems are those associated with the move, with the changes he is having to assimilate and with coping with the new and the different, and what problems are actually to do with his new environment. If the problems are actually to do with his being at the new school, what do you do then?

Managing your child's ongoing education is beyond the scope of this book (although many of the transition strategies given here can be adapted to become strategies to help manage AS in education if the willingness is there). It is, of course, extremely sad if the having successfully made it 'over the bridge' of transition you find the view from the other side less than rosy.

It may be that if this is the case you will need to look at the school and how it manages ongoing support, how ready it is to differentiate for your child's needs, how flexible it is in its approach and how it manages matters such as bullying and discipline within its usual routine. Schools are highly sociably-governed establishments.

Success at them is frequently determined by social skill and status and they can be hostile and intimidating worlds to the vulnerable. Schools have a responsibility to keep all the pupils in their care safe and certainly any bullying or intimidation is a matter for the school to sort out. You and your child have an absolute right to expect this to be managed successfully, and most schools will expend considerable energy and resources on doing so. If you take your concerns to your named adult, and are prepared to work together, there is every chance that the school will be able to resolve these sorts of problems. Put simply, it has to: the school has a responsibility to be a safe place for your child where he is free from intimidation or fear, so problems in this area are, in a sense, the school's, not yours or your child's. Protect your child from problems (by keeping him at home if necessary) until issues have been resolved, and do not accept any suggestion that the school has 'done all it can'. It may take a certain tenacity on your part, but the school can and will sort out bullying, name-calling and other unpleasantness and will certainly be aware that it is there absolute duty to do so, particularly if the child is being victimized or discriminated against because of disability.

More difficult to deal with head on is that too often a child with AS in a school, especially after his initial 'transition' has passed, may almost be expected to adapt to the school's ways and in effect to 'get over' his autism. As someone with an invisible condition, he may find that others gradually forget to make adjustments to allow for his condition, or do not understand the need to make those adjustments, or even (at its worst) that they cease to believe that his condition exists. The effect, if your child is being given no real differentiation to allow for his AS, is that he is likely to find that the task of having AS and managing a school environment for himself is a very difficult one indeed.

Schools are places where learning takes place, and as already discussed in section 4.3 forcing a student to endure what is to him an unsuitable environment may well greatly reduce his potential for learning. Equally, and just as importantly, schools should be teaching a great deal more than what is covered in the academic syllabus. Schools have a responsibility, in their care of young people through these developing years, to help those students to develop a sense of self and of self-worth, of identity and personal responsibility. To ignore the Asperger needs of a person with AS is to ignore the fact of that person having AS. This may not be only to limit the person's ability to function in the neuro-typical world, but is to miss an opportunity to help that person to develop strategies to manage his AS. AS is not something that will go away if no allowances are made for it. Far more likely is that the student, denied the opportunity to develop a coping strategy, will become withdrawn, or distressed and 'difficult', his unhappiness a direct result of not being able to manage his AS.

What is needed is to help the student with AS to understand his condition and to learn to manage it for himself. Simple coping strategies such as leaving classes a little early or being permitted to study individually rather than working in a group allow the student to perfect techniques that will go with him into later life. After all, he can always catch an early or late train into town to avoid the rush hour – but he will still have made the trip to town. He can choose a job that allows him to work from home or via a computer, rather than in an active team. As an adult, he may find any number of ways of avoiding environments that he cannot handle. Only as a child is he likely to be forced into situations that are intolerable. Indeed, as an adult, he will have disability law to help to protect him and help him to facilitate necessary differentiation. It seems very unfair if this is not extended to him while he is a child.

Awareness of his needs must be developed by school staff, of course, but perhaps most importantly it needs to be developed in the student himself. It is vitally important that the student with AS be helped to understand that it is the fact of his having AS that is making dealing with his school environment difficult, and not some failure of intelligence or courage. Understanding who he is and why he is like he is, is the process of growing up that all young people need to address through these years, and is a process that schools are supposed to be helping them to tackle. To expect a young person with AS to be able to make that understanding if the AS is left out of the equation, is to expect him to complete a complex jigsaw puzzle with half the pieces missing.

If your child's unhappiness continues, despite your best efforts of working with him and with the school, it may be that you will need to address these issues for yourself. If the school does not have an existing Asperger community, and if you are struggling to persuade them to allow one to develop, it may be that your child will need help and support from an outside source – from a local autism support group, for example, from autism experts or from an on-line Asperger group. Try to allow your child to understand that the community of the school is hard for him because it is established on neuro-typical lines. However hard the members of the community try to differentiate for him (and they should, indeed, try hard to do so), it may nevertheless never really be an entirely 'suitable' place for him. He needs to be confident that this is not because of some failure on his part, but quite simply because he is in a minority. He has AS and most of the people in the school do not.

If you and he and the school community can accept this, it may well be that your child's school days can be happy and fulfilling. He need not, in other words, be unhappy at school because he has AS. If he is allowed to differentiate for some of the needs that his having AS create, and if he is supported to be able to communicate these needs and for these needs to be taken seriously, it is perfectly possible that he can take full and happy part in all aspects of school life. If he is able to understand his own needs, he will learn how to manage them. If he accepts that much of school is irrelevant, unsuitable or incomprehensible, he may learn to be more tolerant of it.

What is hoped is that, now that he has made this transition to a more senior school environment, he can learn to negotiate this environment for himself and through his time at it, learn what it is to be a happy, fulfilled and successful adult. If he can accept that he will be that adult with AS, and can have come to an understanding of how he will manage – and even celebrate – that fact on into adult life, he will have achieved a great deal indeed. He is not a 'problem', nor is his AS. This on-going transition from child to adult is one that he will make with your help, but that to be successful he will ultimately make away from you.

Your active support in his transition between schools will, I hope, act as a blue-print for you both. If you have managed together to find a way to manage this journey, you will have given him valuable tools to take with him on his next. This will not be the end of his journey, nor even the last time he manages transition – far from it. It does, though, mark a significant step in his journey to independence. Indeed, his next transition is likely to be, formally, to adulthood, whether this be independent living, employment or further education. By making this school move make sense you have, it may be hoped, shown him a way to manage the business of transition, as well as making this transition itself successful. If moving up, and moving on, can be no longer an alarming or overwhelming experience, but can be manageable and can even make sense, then together you have achieved a great deal. You, your child's previous school, his current school, the teachers, support staff, other students and most of all your child himself, have created a considerable achievement, and it is worth taking a moment realize this. Well done!

Appendix: Transition Check-list

When choosing a new school for your child, or perhaps when reviewing what is available at the school you have chosen, the following may be provisions that are worth bearing in mind. No school is likely to offer all of them. They are ideas and examples of best practice gathered from a whole range of schools, and from parents of children with Asperger syndrome and high functioning autism who say that these supports would have helped their child make transition between schools. Not all of these supports will be suitable for all children, nor would all, even, help all children. However, they are a useful 'shopping list' to use to decide what help you think your child could use. You could use the list to see which your child's school is offering, which you would like to request be put into place and, indeed, which you could implement yourself.

Helpful strategies to support the successful transition between schools for pupils with Asperger syndrome

1.   **Visits arranged for the pupil with AS into the new school.** These might be during the school day, after school, with the SENCO, the named adult, with a current 1:1 support or with parents. The pupil could 'shadow' another pupil for part of a day during the final term before the move. He could be allowed regular and open access to the school buildings after school in order to learn the layout, take photographs, etc. The pupil could be supported to experience lunch, the canteen system, etc. and to become familiar with the safe haven available during the unstructured times of the school day. He could become familiar with a variety of classrooms and learning environments. Visits to the school would allow the pupil to become familiar with much of the sensory stimuli of the school environment, for example allowing him to gain experience of such things as school bells, sirens, buzzers and PA systems.

2.   **Visits arranged by the new school to the current school.** As well as more formal visit by, for example, the SENCO to the end of year review, staff from the new school are likely to benefit both from observing the pupil with AS in his current setting and from accessing the expertise that has been built up in that current setting. If the pupil is able to show his new 'named adult' around his current school, this makes for an excellent introduction.

3. **Home visits.** These would allow the SENCO to become familiar with the pupil in a relaxed setting, and allow his parents a greater opportunity to discuss their child's needs in a less potentially intimidating environment. Home visits would allow the SENCO to be aware of the culture, expectations, language and potential support of home. AS crosses all race, religious, ethnic, social and economic borders, and it makes sense for the SENCO (who does not, presumably, have difficulties in flexibility) to be aware of any potential differences between the child's home and school environments.

4. **A 'named adult'.** Someone from the new school should provide a consistent point of contact with pupil and parents throughout the transition. The SENCO may be responsible for the planning of transition, but she may not be the pupil's or the parents' first point of contact once the child has moved schools. It is important that who is the 'named adult' responsible for the child be made clear, and that the child and his parents be able to deal consistently with one person.

5. **Visual supports/paraphernalia.** The new school could provide copies of maps, timetables, planners, exercise books, text books, library cards, swipe cards, etc. Even if these are not relevant for the coming year (the timetable for the new school year may not yet have been finalized), familiarity with the look and layout of materials is likely to be helpful. If possible, the pupil could also be allowed to take photographs around the new school and be provided with photographs of key staff who will be working with

him in the next academic year. Familiarity with 'new' technologies such as swipe cards are likely to reduce anxiety when faced with them in the first days.

6. **A safe haven.** It is imperative that the pupil with AS has somewhere where he can go if in need of sanctuary. Access to this should, ideally, be available at any time on request (and request might be through presentation of an 'Exit Card', since communication skills may be the first to go if the child is under stress). It should be staffed by someone with good AS understanding who understands the ideas behind the room's use. Ideally the pupil with AS would keep some of his possessions here, especially whatever he finds most useful for self-calming (e.g. books around his special interest, card collection, etc.). The safe haven should additionally be available to the pupil during all unstructured times, should he wish to access it.

7. **Support for break/lunch/unstructured time.** As well as access to a safe haven during these times, additional support should be made available to the pupil with AS to enable him to safely/successfully access canteen or dining area, bathrooms and any clubs or leisure-time activities.

8. **A plan for managing movement around school.** This could be through additional adult support, through a pairing or buddy system with another pupil or through allowing the pupil with AS to leave classes early to avoid the crush. It is important that whatever support is put in place, it is kept in place

for as long as the pupil needs it, even though he may now know his way around the site.

9. **Established structures to ensure full multi-way communication during transition** (between old school, new school, autism advisers, parents, child). Problems for the child with AS when changing schools may come about through poor communication. An established and active system is needed that involves accessing the expertise from the previous school, autism outreach advisers, the parents, the SENCO and/or named adult and – importantly – the child himself. With good communication many problems can be avoided, and the burden of articulating difficulties not be made to fall on the child with AS (who is likely to have a diagnosed difficulty in this area).

10. **Contact if desired with other pupils with AS in the school and their parents** (an AS community). If desired, contact with other pupils with AS, and contact for parents of a pupil with AS new to the school with other parents of children with AS already at the school, can be a great source of support. A 'culture of AS' means that problems previously experienced may be avoided, and solutions that have already been found to work may be suggested. For the pupils, greater self-awareness and self-understanding may combat many of the self-esteem issues that result from being 'different'. A mentoring system involving older pupils with AS providing support to younger can have benefit for both. An AS community allows for AS-specific education (for

example, an autism outreach educator to come in to run sessions on puberty and sexual awareness, social interaction, etc.).

11. **Contact/continuity during holidays.** Some access to the school site, or at least to updates on the timetable, changes in staffing and so on, can prevent/lessen the build-up of anxiety over the holiday break. Many school years begin with a teacher-training day that may additionally give an opportunity for the pupil with AS to access the school, visit his form room and meet his form teacher.

12. **Staff who are sensitive to sensory issues.** A school that has good active awareness of these issues is more likely to anticipate problems and allow gradual introduction to certain environments. Ideally the school will have a policy that recognizes that some rooms, and some lessons, are likely to be challenging to the child with AS. It may be best if the pupil is permitted to access the safe haven as an alternative to the crowded assembly hall, the echoing gymnasium, the strongly smelling Science labs or the blacked-out Drama studio, at least until he has had a chance to settle at the school. Staff should be aware that how he 'manages' may not be a reflection of his sensory distress, and that non-disruptive behaviour must never be taken to mean a lack of need (since, at very least, all this will teach him is that he needs to be disruptive if he is to escape from a stressful environment).

13. **Secure understanding of the basic needs of the child with AS** (eating/toileting/safety, etc.). The pupil's basic safety needs, his physical and hygiene needs must be met if he is to make a successful transition. It may be accepted that the other pupils are able to make their way safely to, for example, a sports field, crossing a number of roads – but if the pupil with AS does not have sufficient road-safety understanding, this must not be accepted for him. Similarly, it may be necessary to have provision in place in case of accidents, soiling, etc. The sensitive and speedy handling of a situation such as this can make a huge difference to the long-term emotional impact it is likely to have on the pupil.

14. **Technology support.** If a pupil has difficulty with handwriting, a lap-top or 'word harvester'-type word processor can make a huge difference. If he is struggling, organizationally, to manage the day then a diary-computer programmed with prompts can help enormously. Being able to text to the SENCO or other adult support when in need of help can be a life line. E-mail clarification of a homework task can prevent confusion and help achievement. Technology can be the greatest support in managing this transition, but it needs to be recognized, and accepted, by all parties.

15. **Whole-school understanding of AS** (differentiated teaching, not just TA support). Too much emphasis can be placed by some schools on support offered by TAs and learning support staff. Although these adults may have a part to play in helping the child with

AS through this transition, their presence does not negate the teachers' and the school's responsibilities to differentiate for the pupil's needs. Successful transition is far more likely if there is whole-school understanding of AS. The learning of the pupil with AS should be delivered by the teacher in a way that suits his learning style and which meets his special educational needs; his safety, happiness and overall welfare are the responsibility of all staff – teachers, headteacher, education board, etc. – not just of the special needs department.

16. **AS-aware support to help the child understand problems in transition.** Problems experienced during transition are less likely to have a serious effect on a child if the staff who are managing the transition are AS aware. If difficulties that arise can be interpreted by someone with good autism understanding, both the cause and the solution are more likely to be appropriate to the child with AS. Neuro-typical interpretations of events may not be relevant, or even helpful. Someone to help the pupil who has good AS understanding will not just help him through this transition, but help him more widely to understand his condition and himself.

17. **A flexi-start.** One way to make the transition to the new school less overwhelming is to consider a flexi-start. This allows for a more gradual introduction to the school – perhaps mornings only to begin with, or with a 'day off' midweek. This can work for a number of reasons. Shorter periods of time in school can lead to the new school being less overwhelming.

This in turn can lead to more successful coping by the child with AS, and less risk of disruptive or unusual behaviour (which itself carries a risk of peer-rejection). It allows for more time for his parents or an autism adviser to work with the child and explain and explore the challenges that are being faced. It respects the child's need for time alone or to pursue a special interest and 'self-repair'. It also flags up the different-ness of the child with AS, and therefore makes it unnecessary for his peers to do so. Much of the rejection and taunting of children with AS is because they are identified by their peers as being 'odd' or 'weird'. Identifying difference openly can reduce the need for it to be pointed out during this difficult initial period, when the social pecking-order is being established and even the stronger individuals cannot allow themselves to be allied with the 'weak'. Once social status has been established, those with high social standing are far more likely to be in a position to offer kindness and even protection to the more vulnerable.

18. **Previous AS transition feedback.** Your child is unlikely to be the first with AS to have made the transition to the school. Feedback on what transition support has been previously put in place should be available, together with evaluation of that transition from staff, parents and the pupil. Feedback about what works best is essential if the feeder schools are to make the best provision during their time, and evaluation of what works and what does not (especially if the reasons are understood) should mean that the same mistakes are not repeated with

each new pupil with an ASD. It is important that feedback is sought actively from the pupil, and in a way that is meaningful to him. Using 1:1 interview/ questioning may not be the best way to allow him to identify his needs. Questionnaires, computer-based surveys, opportunities to visually record fears, discomfort, anxieties and confusions should all be explored if we are all to learn from the experience of those going through school transition with AS.

19. **Adaptability and flexibility.** It is quite likely that, by definition, the young person with AS is going to find adaptability and flexibility an issue. It may well be necessary, then, for those around him to compensate for this by being both adaptable and flexible themselves. To a great extent, the transition of the pupil with AS will be made easier if those around him (who do not have AS) are prepared to adapt their behaviour, communication style, social attitudes, behavioural expectations and educational approaches to allow for his AS. Although this is pretty much self-obvious, the school's willingness to be flexible may be something that you need to discuss with them. Your child's transition is going to be a whole lot easier if he does not come up against a 'This is how we do it here' attitude that allows for no adaptability. The school will have its set of rules ('pupils are expected to...'), but is it able to waiver or adapt those rules and expectations as necessary in order to provide inclusion for a pupil with AS?

20. **Enthusiasm for your child and his needs, both as a person with AS and as an individual.** If the school can see no further than the 'problem' of a pupil having AS, it is unlikely the staff involved will be able to enjoy having him as a member of their community. There is a huge amount in AS that is fascinating, rewarding, amusing, intriguing and beneficial to a school, and an individual with AS is a great deal more than his diagnosis. If staff are weary or fearful about other aspects of their jobs they may not be able to provide the best for your child, nor to get the best out of having him in their community. If they are interested and enthusiastic, excited by the adventure and ready to work together to make the very best of the journey, then they can make this work…and it can be a great experience for everybody.

Further Reading

Al-Ghani, K.I. and Kenward, L. (2009) *Making the Move: A Guide for Schools and Parents on the Transfer of Pupils with ASD from Primary to Secondary School.* London: Jessica Kingsley Publishers.

Attwood, T. (2007) *The Complete Guide to Asperger Syndrome.* London: Jessica Kingsley Publishers.

Beaney, J. and Kershaw, P. (2006) *Inclusion in the Secondary School: Support Materials for Children with Autistic Spectrum Disorders.* London: National Autistic Society.

Bolick, T. (2001) *Asperger Syndrome and Adolescence: Helping Pre-teens and Teens get Ready for the Real World.* Minneapolis: Fair Winds Press.

Broderick, K. and Mason-Willimas, T. (2008) *Transition Toolkit.* Kidderminster: British Institute of Learning Difficulties.

Colley, J. (2005) *Working with an Asperger Pupil in Secondary Schools.* London: National Autistic Society.

Dubin, N. (2007) *Asperger Syndrome and Bullying: Strategies and Solutions.* London: Jessica Kingsley Publishers.

Jackson, L. (2002) *Freaks, Geeks and Asperger Syndrome: A User Guide to Adolescence.* London: Jessica Kingsley Publishers.

Jackson, L. (2003) *Asperger Syndrome in the Adolescent Years: Living with the Ups, the Downs and Things in Between.* London: Jessica Kingsley Publishers.

Lawrence, C. (2008) *How to Make School Make Sense.* London: Jessica Kingsley Publishers.

Leicestershire County Council (1998) *Asperger Syndrome - Practical Strategies for the Classroom: A Teacher's Guide.* London: National Autistic Society.

Murray, D. (2006) (ed.) *Coming Out Asperger: Diagnosis, Disclosure and Self Confidence.* London: Jessica Kingsley Publishers.

National Autistic Society (2005) *Autistic Spectrum Disorders: A Guide for Secondary Schools.* London: National Autistic Society.

Sainsbury, S. (2000) *Martian in the Playground.* London: Jessica Kingsley Publishers.

Sicile-Kira, C. (2006) *Adolescents on the Autistic Spectrum.* London: Random House.

Smith Myles, B. and Adreon, D. (2001) *Asperger Syndrome and Adolescence: Practical Solutions for School Success.* London: Jessica Kingsley Publishers.

South Gloucestershire Council (2005) *Guidelines for Working with Pupils with an ASD in Key Stages 3 and 4.* London: National Autistic Society.

Thorpe, P. (2004) ASD Guides: *Moving from Primary to Secondary School; Understanding Difficulties at Break Time and Lunchtime; Bullying and How to Deal with it.* London: National Autistic Society.